The World Needs Dialogue!

Five: Dialogue as Story

Dialogue
Publications

This edition first published in 2023

Dialogue Publications
The Firs, High Street, Chipping Campden
Glos GL55 6AL UK

Typeset by Ellipsis, Glasgow, Scotland

Ordering Information:

Quantity sales – Special discounts are available on quantity purchases by libraries, associations
and others. For details, contact the Special Sales Department at the address above.

The World Needs Dialogue! / Five – 1st ed.

Classifications:
UK: BIC – Society (JFC): Cultural Studies and JFF: Social Issues)
US: BISAC – SOC000000 Social Science

ISBN Hardback: 978-1-7384072-0-0
ISBN Ebook: 978-1-7399911-9-7

Printed in Great Britain and the USA

On the Cover:
*The cover photo depicts the challenge of making coherent sense of the world, given the continuous
stream of informing data and opinions from publications, media and social media.
Dialogue as Story offers a way of placing things within the context of one's own first-hand
experience and personal knowledge.*

Contents

Trustee's Foreword

Dialogue as Story was the fifth annual conference of the Academy of Professional Dialogue and, like this publication, broke new ground in the territory it explored. Once again there was a remarkable turnout of more than 300 people from 24 different countries, gathered in the Academy's online conference centre for a fascinating participatory event.

The theme, of both the conference and this book, is wide-ranging. The simple notion is that we naturally make sense of the world around us through stories, joining apparently disparate pieces of information into a single narrative, or building a big picture from a small piece of information. Groups of people with a common storyline share a subcultural identity, which affects how they make sense. Large organisations have a storyline created and sustained collectively by many people within the organisation, and those who hold the reputation from the outside. There are so many stories and storylines weaving through this book.

The storyline of the Academy itself now covers seven years since its inception in 2016, developing as an educational charity and professional body for practitioners working with Professional Dialogue. The aim of the Academy is to inspire people to use Professional Dialogue, acknowledge practitioners for their good work, provide an educational and developmental path, and develop the whole field of Professional Dialogue work. The 2022 conference focused for the first time on the latter, as participants were invited to step into an experience of becoming aware of their stories and storylines, noticing their impact and adding to the collective learning. This book, under the wise eye of the editor, Peter Garrett, brings that rich experience into written form to share.

Whilst previous Academy conference publications* have included carefully written papers and case studies about work that has been done, this publication marks a lively departure from that format. The process itself comes alive here, as well as the content. Rather than an author's story about what happened in the past and what they learnt, we hear insights through the words of the four plenary facilitators, 31 participatory dialogue facilitators, and the majority of the 315 participants – voices from 24 different countries. The narrative is largely taken from transcripts, which are engaging and convey the participatory nature of the conference, and the live learning that took place.

The book is not only about the different voices. Within the engaging dynamic is a strong structure that grounds the theory that is being explicated here. The plenary sessions reveal Dialogue as Story for **me,** or the self; for **us** within subcultural groups; for **organisations**; and for the **world**, with a global perspective. The plenary facilitators draw participants to

---

* See the Dialogue Publications catalogue: *TWND! One: Gathering the Field* (2019), *TWND! Two: Setting the Bearings* (2020), *TWND! Three: Shaping the Profession* (2021), *TWND! Four: Putting Dialogue to Work* (2022).

consider: What are the many versions of me and how do they affect what I say and do? How do all the groups I identify with affect the way I think and participate? The organizational perspective is revealed directly through the lens of four generations from Virginia Department of Corrections. This story also shows how Dialogue has enabled their culture to hold these different stories in a generative common storyline.

The one paper that was brought into the conference is at the heart of the book – the formative writings by Peter Garrett on Dialogue as Story. This is a great stand-alone read, which provides a theoretical context, relating Dialogue as Story to the underlying ontology of Professional Dialogue from David Bohm. It also introduces the distinction I have mentioned between the immediate sense-making of stories and the enduring and influential nature of storylines.

The third part of the book offers a broad range of stimulating ideas. Each day participants were able to join a Participatory Dialogue 'where everyone learns, and nobody teaches'. The stories of 19 Participatory Dialogues are told through the voices of their facilitators and participants. Each one includes an introduction from the facilitators explaining why they chose the topic, a transcript of spontaneous closing comments from each session participant about what they learnt, and a reflective conclusion written by the facilitators sometime later.

In Section One there are four such descriptions of enquiries about Self that raise worthwhile questions for us all to consider. Why do we ignore parts of ourselves we don't like, or exclude our personal identity at work? How do we ever notice the parts of our identity we ignore, and how does Dialogue enable an integration of all of us? A standout session explores how the storylines of both victims and offenders become stuck as the result of an offence, and a dialogic process that brings them together provides both with a generative way forward.

Three sessions in Section Two delve into subcultural fragmentation, and the impact of diverging storylines, social media and its echo chambers. This theme is brought out by a consideration of the experience migrants have when they return to their home, and another on the divisive subject of race and policing in the US.

Section Three goes on to Participatory Dialogues with an organisational context. These consider the barriers created by our stories about others in organisations, because of hierarchy, power difference, role, or as teacher and student, and how this can be overcome. I would like to make a special mention of Matt Burgess, whose session is included in this section. Matt was a dedicated Dialogue Practitioner at Virginia Department of Corrections from 2014, and sadly passed away in December 2022. His enquiry into the impact of the unforgiving storylines communities hold about offenders was characteristically courageous.

At a social level, three sessions in Section Four consider the storylines arising from the larger forces in our lives – being a woman, the gap between different generations and how to find meaning in life itself.

Finally, in Section Five, we can read about five sessions that explored qualities of facilitation and participation that might be needed to enable storylines to shift in a Dialogue. Power, pace and silence, what is said and not said, are all thought-provoking themes for a practitioner. I hope these descriptions have given you a feel for the richness of this genuinely collaborative publication.

Within this richness lies a crucial central message. The lives of many of us have become complex and scattered. We have access to so much information, much of it online and fed to us by algorithms. Often, we don't know the source, or what is true. In this state, we are left like the young man on the cover of this book – struggling to make sense of everything we are told and looking deeper into our devices for the answer. Dialogue is more necessary than ever to help us to find that coherent storyline, and halt the breakup of our organisations, communities and perhaps our very selves.

Jane Ball
Trustee and Founding Director
Academy of Professional Dialogue

Editor's Preface

Every year the Academy's international conference has the bold but self-evidently true title **The World Needs Dialogue!** This year's innovative theme was *Dialogue as Story*. For context, the formative writing by me that led to the conference theme is included in this volume. It opened plenty of space for fresh thinking.

Over 300 individuals from 24 countries met each day in parallel 90-minutes break-out Participatory Dialogues to consider different topics related to the main theme. The focus of these sessions incorporated a broad array of issues like identity (individual and collective), the privilege of gender, the generation gap, violent crime, policing deaths, the impact of power dynamics and the value of silence. We have published extracts and reflections from half of those 38 co-facilitated sessions.

In addition, during each day there were plenary presentations made by four seasoned Professional Dialogue Practitioners. Their interactive sessions explored *Dialogue as Story* at the level of **me** (Peter Garrett), **us** (Jane Ball), the **organization** (Harold Clarke) and the **world** (William Isaacs). They clearly deepened the content and enriched the theoretical understanding of the convention. It is worth noting that these four individuals know each other well and have been colleagues and friends since before the turn of the century. They represent the living foundation stones of Professional Dialogue and the weight of this book rests on their shoulders. They carry the responsibility lightly and with enthusiasm.

Jane Ball accepted the invitation to write the Foreword for this book, a role that I have played for the past volumes. As a Founding Director of the Academy of Professional Dialogue, a current Trustee and an eloquent writer, Jane is particularly well-suited to open this new volume.

Editing the book is a year-long process, culminating in publication at the following year's conference. Although Cliff Penwell vacated the role of editor in 2022, at which point I assumed that position, he has remained helpfully present in the background. I am grateful to have been very ably supported by Helena Wagener who is the copy editor for this book, and I appreciate the administrative support from Natalia Sobrino-Saeb, Bethany Smith and Bobby Frazier. Debi Letham of Ellipsis Books designed the cover and has managed the book's layout and typesetting, as she has done so well for our entire series. You may choose to note the significance of the blue cover of this year's book. Previous volumes have been red, then orange, yellow and green. As you can see, we are following the colours of the rainbow. I am very curious to see how indigo and violet fare over the next two years!

Peter Garrett
Editor, Dialogue Publications

Dialogue as Story

Introduction

The Academy broke new ground with its fifth annual international conference in 2022 by considering a new way of experiencing Dialogue: *Dialogue as Story*. Participants had the opportunity to extend and deepen their understanding through a participatory exploration of this innovative perspective on Dialogue.

People may be more familiar with *Dialogue as a Mode*, which is distinct from monologue, discussion, debate, conversation and so on. Others have concentrated on the experience of *Dialogue as a Practice,* involving a lifelong journey with voice, listening, respect and suspension. Those who work primarily in organizations may have drawn on *Dialogue as a Process*, where everyone has a voice in generating a common understanding that provides a context for better decision-making. *Dialogue as Story* is not intended as a replacement for these more familiar ways of conceiving of Dialogue but as an addition to them.

The aim of the conference was not to encourage storytelling. That is an art best conveyed through monologue, not Dialogue. Nor was there the proposal that we should try to invent new stories. The aim was to go a level deeper to see what is already happening. We wanted to give attention to the unnoticed way human consciousness works – by making sense of things through the form of story. It is a fundamental part of how we think, feel and act.

Depending on their history and perspective, people in the same situation often hold well-constructed but different stories about what is happening. This is commonly experienced as the disjointed or fragmented state in society and in organizations. Dialogue, then, is the generative process by which we can understand, refine and incorporate the many versions of reality into a mutually inclusive and commonly held story. This is a *living* story in which everyone has played, and continues to play, a meaningful part. In this way, *Dialogue as Story* provides a means of moving beyond social and organisational fragmentation. By attending to the collective story, Dialogue generates broad understanding and aligned meaning. It also generates the fabric of interrelated identities that have a sense of fellowship and citizenship.

This volume explores *Dialogue as Story* in three parts:

The first part of the book describes the plenary input during the conference where *Dialogue as Story* was explored at four different levels:

- **me** (the self) introduced by Peter Garrett
- **us** (the subculture) introduced by Jane Ball
- **the organization** introduced by Harold Clarke
- **the world** (society) introduced by William Isaacs.

The second part covers the underlying theory and background thinking that led to *Dialogue as Story* being proposed as the theme for this conference.

The third part reveals some of the exploration by participants in 19 co-facilitated Participatory Dialogues (each lasting 90 minutes) held during the conference. Towards the close of each Participatory Dialogue, the check-out (or closing round of reflective comments) was recorded and transcribed. Later, the co-facilitators were invited to write a postscript reflecting on their own learning during their Participatory Dialogue and in relation to the conference theme, *Dialogue as Story*.

PART ONE

PLENARY CONFERENCE SESSIONS

Dialogue as Story: Self

Peter Garrett

Giuseppe Verdi's 'La Traviata' was playing as people gathered.

Jane Ball: Welcome to the second day of our conference. That was wonderful classical music and singing – one of my favorite operas. Yesterday we talked about stories and storylines. We just heard an extract, a duet, but that opera has a storyline. It is about two people who fall in love; there's some confusion about their commitment to each other and it all ends tragically. That tragedy uses a storyline that has played out in many stories throughout history, and in lots of different modern movies. It shows how a storyline repeats itself in lots of different forms, different stories. There are many stories and far fewer storylines.

Today we're going to go into the theme Dialogue As Story in more depth, looking through four different lenses. First the self with Peter, then us as a group with me, the organization with Harold Clarke and then the world with Bill Isaacs. With that, I'm going to hand it over to you, Peter.

Peter: Good morning, good afternoon, good evening, depending on where you are! Yesterday I did an overview of Dialogue As Story. Let's do a recap. What I proposed is that there are different ways of considering Dialogue.

One is Dialogue as a Mode. Clearly Dialogue is different from monologue. A check-in is a series of monologues. It's not a dialogue. Debate is different, and Discussion is different from Dialogue. Dialogue has some very special qualities. For example, it enables difference to be accommodated in a remarkably generative way. Understanding the value of all the modes, and Dialogue as a Mode is one approach.

Secondly, I described Dialogue as a Practice. Voice, listening, respect and suspension. A lifelong practice of how to engage with others, understand others and yourself and how to talk and think together. Dialogue as a Practice is a different way of coming at dialogue.

And then I described a third one, Dialogue as a Process. In organizational and community activities this means that those who are affected by a decision have a voice and can participate in the decision-making process. This is not a consensus model. It's more about trying to understand the impact a decision may have on everyone before making it. How do we all do this well, taking the whole into account?

We have Dialogue as a Process, Dialogue as a Practice, and Dialogue as a Mode. They are all interrelated. If you master these three, you can do intervention work. You can go into an organization or community where there is a problem that's stuck and won't shift, and you can move it. You will be able to do organizational intervention work.

A reminder that the roots of the word Dialogue are dia, meaning 'through', and logos, meaning 'the word', so Dialogue is a common meaning or a common understanding amongst a group of people. We don't have to make all our decisions sitting down together. We can each make our decisions in our own area, but through Dialogue we all understand what we're doing and trying to do, and how what I do will be of help to the overall movement. That's the idea around having a common understanding or a common meaning.

It was David Bohm who pointed out that we have a widespread problem of fragmentation, where people don't have a common understanding. Why does it matter? If we don't have a common understanding, we inadvertently trip each other up. We do things that don't help one another without necessarily realising that we're being unhelpful. We can do it deliberately too, but mainly it is good people inadvertently tripping each other up.

This is where Dialogue as Story comes in. I described story-making as an automatic process. It's very quick. So quick we don't notice it occurring. It is how we make sense of things. Something happens and immediately I have a story about what happened. We also looked at the storyline. Jane referred to it as we began today's session. The storyline is the meaning underneath the story. There are few storylines and lots of stories. We're saying that if we have the same storyline, the stories we have create a welcome diversity. Perhaps we all thought it was a great event, and we each have our different stories of how and why it was a great event. If we have fundamentally different storylines, however, we have fragmentation. We have the problem that all our stories don't fit together. We can work very hard, experiencing some conflict, trying to compromise to get them to fit together. The idea of Dialogue as Story is to get below the storyline and see how the storylines are working. So that's a little recap of yesterday.

I would like to continue by exploring Dialogue as Story in relation to oneself. Would you like to try a little experiential learning exercise? Are you willing to try it? What that means is we try something and afterwards we reflect on what happened and what we discovered or learned. OK. We're going to break out into trios – groups of three people. The exercise is in several parts that won't all be done at once. The first part is, in your group of three people, I want one of you to ask one of the others, Who are you? and that person responds. You do not need any preliminary introductions for this exercise. It may be somebody you know or somebody you do not know, but the question is, Who are you? and the person answers the question. Each person takes a turn. So, when the first person has finished, someone asks one of the others, Who are you? Not, How are you? or, Where are you or anything else! Just Who are you? We will give you six or seven minutes. Each have a turn, and the aim is to watch what happens. Notice if you're keen to go first or last, or whatever. Just have the experience. Good luck if you're looking forward to it! If you're not, you'll probably learn even more. So, let's find out.

Participants go to break-out rooms for six minutes.

Peter: Good. Welcome back. What was your experience?

Speaker: That's always a hard question. I was telling my group that's always a difficult question for me to answer because it really makes me have a good look at myself. Sometimes I don't know how to answer that. I don't know whether to answer with personality traits or what. I think I just answered with, I really like my job. I'm a job-oriented person. That's kind of who I am. So, yeah, it was a difficult question for me personally.

Peter: I agree. I tried it as well... Another comment. What was your experience doing that?

Speaker: We were having a very interesting discussion, and we didn't want to come back here. We wanted to extend it a little longer.

Speaker: Peter, this is Harold. I'll just add that the question helps you to realise that you're a lot more than you think you are – a lot more than you may think of at any given time.

Peter: Good, Harold. I noticed in the trio I was in, people paused trying to answer the question. It wasn't straightforward. It took a little bit of thinking. How should I answer this question?

All right, now for the second part of our exercise. Bobby, please get ready to drop us back again into trios, but different trios. The question to answer in this new trio is the question, Who are you? You'll notice it's the same question you've already answered. I want you to repeat the exercise with a new group, Who are you? One person asks another, hears the answer, and goes around. All three of you answer the same question. There is one difference, however. The elements of the little story you told about yourself – don't repeat any of them. Don't repeat the story you told. You'll notice there's more than one story inside you about who you are. You may have put several of them in your previous answer. Try letting go of those and find another answer to the question, Who are you? Without using the same ideas or referencing the same thoughts you did previously. If you described your role, your experience, or your family – leave them out this time. Don't make up a story, a false one. There are plenty of true ones in there. So, Bobby, into new trios for the same time and for the same exercise but with a different story.

Peter: Welcome back. The idea of the experiential learning exercise was to learn something about yourself. How did you find the second round? The same exercise, but not using the same story, the same identity. Any comments? Come in when you're ready.

Speaker: I felt like this time, in the second go-around, it was easier than the first go-around, but you had to dig a little deeper. You had to think a little more on the second go-around.

Speaker: The first time around, I was giving examples of who I was in comparison to the people I'm close to. I was like, I'm a mother, I'm a twin, I'm a daughter. But in this round, I was thinking I'm way more than that. I started speaking about my character and my future. It was a deeper insight about myself.

Speaker: Like Mr. Clarke said, you learn that you are a lot more than you realise. I went first in the first round, and I said some things. Then as the group went round, I thought, Oh, I could have said that, and I could also have said that. So, the second time around I went first again, and I included some of those things – but then when the other two went I was like, Ah, I could have said that too, and I could have said that too! You learn more and more about yourself each time.

Peter: And one last one Karen.

Speaker: It was a little bit more challenging for me the second time because I thought I had given the answer the first time. I thought I was very clear, and I gave all the things that I felt I am. But then the second time was like, Okay, now I have to really think about it. Is what I said at first really me? Quite challenging.

Peter: Good. Thank you for all the comments. If we chose to, we could do the same exercise yet again, putting you in another trio with the same question, but not using the answer you gave before. We could keep going in that way and you would find you do go a bit deeper each time into the question, 'Who am I?' The discovery is that identity is a story. It's not a thing, it is a story. You'll notice that your story depends on the situation and the people you are with. If you were quite sharp, you would notice that you chose an answer that made sense on the second day of a conference, and with two other conference participants, whom you may or may not have known.

I happened to know one of the people in my trio, so I shifted my answer a bit. The point I'm making is that the answer is a story, and that you read the situation to come up with a story. The story comes automatically. There it is. It's a little harder when you can't re-use that story which comes automatically. You have to think a little bit more. All the time we are finding and authoring stories. You created a story for your answer. Was it true? Yes. Could you have other versions? Absolutely. There are a large number of stories inside you and me about who I am, and how I have changed. Of course, we'll find, as we move into the next part with Jane, that who we are also depends on the grouping we're in.

One feature is that those stories have a storyline under the story, under your true answers. Who would you like people to see you as? You weren't talking to a tape recorder; you were talking to two other people. You were choosing to be seen in a particular way. The first answer might have been habit. By the second round, you are choosing to be seen in a way. How did you choose to be seen? That's the underlying storyline. Did you choose to be seen as professional, as knowledgeable, as an amateur? Confident? Uncertain? How did you choose to put yourself forward? There's no right way to do this. This is an inquiry. All my life, and all your life, we're doing it. I have an underlying story that I'm representing again and again with every grouping in different ways. Here is a chance to get to know a little more about who I am, and to reflect on that.

That storyline is key to my behavior. If you want to coach me, you will want to notice the storyline underneath my stories. You may remember the Charlie Chaplin movie extract we watched yesterday. He had the bill to pay in the restaurant. It was taken away, then he took it back. It went backwards and forwards. If we coached Charlie Chaplin, we could say, You did it too many times. You should have stopped sooner, and then the artist would have paid the bill. If you went for the storyline, however, you would be thinking, Why are you in that role, Charlie Chaplin? Are you trying to deceive people? Why are you trying to make it look like you have the money to pay when you don't? What is the storyline in you? Who are you trying to impress – your girlfriend, the artist, the waiter, the world? The storyline is the root of all the stories. It is underneath the story of a bill moving backwards and forwards. So, the invitation from Dialogue as Story is to recognise that we create stories every day based on an underlying storyline, and working with the storyline is how we help each other.

Dialogue as Story: Us

Jane Ball

Jane: Of course, if we understand the storyline, we can help each other to shift that storyline. Otherwise, we go back to where we were. That's clear. I was thinking that one of my underlying storylines is that I continually try to do more than I'm able to in the time available. If anyone's willing to coach me on that, I'd be very grateful. I'm already thinking, how will I do everything that I'm planning to do in the next 30 minutes, which is now only 25 minutes – but let's see how we get on. We've just finished talking about ourselves by responding to the question, *Who are You?* The next question then is about the stories and storylines that groups or groupings of people have. These are stories and storylines that we have in common with other people.

I will call them groupings. A grouping sounds like a label, but I'm not talking about a label. I am talking about 'us' as what I call a subcultural grouping, or a grouping of people who have some experience in common. People in a subcultural grouping have common reference points, maybe some common language or ways of talking about things, and a common disposition. That's what I'm talking about when referring to 'us' in Dialogue as Story. To reveal this, I have asked for some volunteers – I invited some people I know to help me to reveal what this looks like. If you are one of my volunteers, please click on the 'reactions' icon at the bottom of the screen to raise your hand. Now Bobby's going to spotlight my first grouping.

Who is this grouping that I invited? Who are we? This is a group of people here at the conference for whom English is not their first language. There are a lot of different subgroups at this conference. For example, we know there is a grouping of Participatory Dialogue facilitators, and we know there's a big Virginia subgroup or subculture. But I wanted to have the opportunity to hear from some people that I think we don't always hear from so much. I'd like to pose a question to you all who are spotlighted, and you can answer in whichever language you would prefer. What is your experience of the conference so far? I feel that it is quite an Anglo-American kind of conference. What's your experience? Some nodding. What do you think?

Speaker: Well, for me it has been a topic since the first conference. Although I would say I'm quite fluent in English, it's still totally different. This year I'm facilitating in English and that gives me a lot of excitement. Sometimes when people are sharing their experiences, they're talking very fast and with different accents and stuff like that. So, I'm pretty aware that I'm not an English-speaking person in this English-speaking conference.

Speaker: Well, despite these differences I feel very comfortable because I know that people can understand the differences between us. It's very interesting for me to talk with different people from different cultures, and about the conference, I love the title of the conference. It is very new. It is very new. So, uh, and makes me all the time thinking about the story and what is going on in the beliefs.

Jane: Can we hear a couple of other voices?

Speaker: I hear the story of passion. I hear that we are all passionate about something, and it also seems that we are passionate about others.

Speaker: I think it's been inspiring, as before. I have been at the conference twice before. It is very inspiring to see people from all around the world who share my passion for Dialogue. I don't have so much problems with the language. I do feel that I'm not completely used to being in this community. I mean, we meet once a year and for me that's mostly all. I think I'm less active in conversations than I would be in a community of people that I meet with regularly. I'm a fairly slow thinker, and I think a difference between the Anglo-Saxon culture and the Swedish one is that there's more rapid conversation and less pauses between the talking, and so on. If I get less involved, it is for that reason.

Speaker: I'd like to follow that because it's the same for me. I think this is a great opportunity to speak with other people and learn from them. I don't have trouble with the language either, but I need to think first before I can answer anything or translate it to myself. That's the problem for me.

Jane: Thank you. It seems very rude (maybe it is an English thing I have about feeling rude) that I'm going to cut you all off at this point. I know we have talked before about how fast-speaking Anglo-Saxons like me could slow down and be a bit more thoughtful. So this is not only a story of this conference, it is a storyline that we've had every year. It's a good reminder to see you all here and to hear your story of the conference so far. Thank you. Bobby will take the spotlight off you, and she'll bring up another grouping that may have a different story.

A few people are staying, and we're going to find a few more people. Then we will see who this next grouping is. Hello. Hi. Good morning! Now I'm getting excited, and I know I must not speak too quickly. This is a different subcultural grouping at our conference. You have probably noticed this is a group of women. Rather than just talking about the conference, I wondered if here we might talk about our story about what it's like being a woman, either at home or in the workplace. I certainly have an experience of that. Maybe we could hear a few comments about that. What's our story of being a woman in the world today?

Speaker: I think that we can all say that it's busy. It's really busy as a woman at home and at work and finding that balance. I am a new grandmother, so that is another role that I have taken on, and I have an only child, so it's just like I have another child. Motherhood has come back, you know, as I play with an infant. It's hectic. Going back to the language barrier, I'm from southwest Virginia and I have a very thick accent. A lot of times it's like I'm speaking a foreign language. Even people who speak English are asking, *What did you say?* So, I understand, and thank you for bringing it to our attention. We do need to slow down sometimes. I also think it's important to say that, with the title of the conference this year, we all have a story. One thing that we have in common is Dialogue. Dialogue is all our stories.

Jane: Very true. What other experiences do other people have of being a woman in our world today?

Speaker: I can relate to being busy, and I'll steal something from our experiential learning where one woman said *I'm a provider*. It struck me that I'm not only providing as a woman for my family, and for my community, but also in my work. I'm a teammate, I'm a support system. I'm a leader and so I just own and love the idea of being a provider.

Speaker: I follow everyone as far as being busy and finding balance since as a woman I am a single mother who has a very demanding career. It's very difficult at times to find balance. As a woman, I try to be conscious of stereotypes because some women can be stereotyped as emotional or things like that. I try to maintain professionalism and to make sure that my outside-of-work life doesn't affect what I have going on at work – even though it's hard to separate the two. But we do it every day, and we make it work. We provide, we have careers, and we take care of the home.

Speaker: It's interesting because I've been reflecting on that question with some women lately. I found out something about myself – that I've not been providing as much as I've heard from others here. I have no children. I dedicate everything to business and being a business owner. I feel that I have learned that I put a lot of effort into learning how to play the male game – If there is a male game, and I'm talking stereotypes here. Just the effort of fitting in and adapting myself to a mostly male environment. It's very interesting for me to go into that question and to sit with women once more. Having met a few great women, a lot of great women, sharing that with me has really changed the way I look at the question.

Speaker: Our culture is changing, and women have been changing. Women become much more every day with the change. Every day they create a new story. And in this story, women help others, and even men to have . . .

Jane: I really want to hear your words, but your internet is poor. Could you type your words into the chat? In a moment I'll read your words out because I know everybody would like to hear them. Certainly, I do. I know that if we had longer we could go to a different depth, but now Bobby is going to let some people go, some will stay and others come to form another grouping. Thank you.

Okay. This is cool. This grouping is a subcultural grouping from the Virginia Department of Corrections, as I think everyone will see. My question to you is, *What is it like working at the Virginia Department of Corrections?* And by that I mean, *What's the story that staff in the Department tell their neighbors, their friends, maybe people at church? What do you say about working in the Department?* I know that your boss, or your boss's boss is listening, but give us an idea anyway. *What's that story?*

Speaker: I have my 34-year anniversary, and I say the Department is a wonderful place to work. The opportunities for promotion, the benefits, the relationships, make it just a wonderful place to work.

Speaker: I will follow my dear friend and coworker. We've been around for years. I've just celebrated 39 years with the Department, and it has been a great provider for me. I enjoy work, and doing what I do every day.

Speaker: Well, I have only 28 years, so I can't relate to that! But I think we have a storyline about public safety and folks can choose what that means to them. I talk about the fact that we incarcerate folks who have decided not to be responsible in society anymore, and that's important. I encourage other folks to do that as well, because in the public, if you're in a store, barbershop or wherever, that's the first thing they want to talk about. Then the education, the treatment and the mental health work and so many things that we do beyond that. It really sparks more conversation with people. They often say, *Oh, I had no idea that you did that!* I think that's the bigger storyline.

Jane: There's more to it than people know, isn't there?

Speaker: I follow the warden that our story is that we're changing lives. Maybe the old story was that we were keeping the public safe, but now we're keeping the public safe *and* we're changing lives. Every day we're learning new things and doing new things, such as the Victim Witness Dialogues we heard about yesterday. Who would've known that you could change both the offender and the victim that way? Every day we're thinking about how we can impact more lives today.

Jane: Good. I can see people agree with that. In that case, I'm going to change to our last grouping. Thank you, Virginia Department of Corrections group. Bye-bye! Maybe some in the conference view the people from the Virginia Department of Corrections as all the same, but I know there are many different subgroups within the Department, each of which has different stories. We're just going to see a final one. And who is this grouping? Do you know who you are? You are all from the Virginia Department of Corrections, and all work in Community Corrections. What's your story? If you imagine that I came to work in your district in Community Corrections, what would you tell me as your new coworker? Over a coffee, what would you say it's like here?

Speaker: I always tell people there's never a dull day. Whether it be in the mental health department or security, there's always something that's keeping you hopping.

Speaker: I always tell people that it's a real good opportunity to witness change. You see the probationers when they come into our facility, you watch them as they go through treatment and educational programs, and by the time they leave, you see how they gain weight, look different and act differently. That's one thing I appreciate, and I tell everybody it's a really good place to witness that change.

Jane: So, I'm going to enjoy my new job?

Speaker: Yes. I'll follow what he just said. It's a great environment to work in, a great learning experience and you can witness the change. If you go to a restaurant in town, you can see your probationers employed and doing great things. I live in the area that I supervise, so I'm directly impacted by the work that I do because I want them to be better. I want them to make better choices. Their kids are going to school with my children. You can really see the impact and the full effect, and it makes you feel good, makes you feel proud to be a part of that process.

Jane: That's a bit different from working in the headquarters or the facilities. You're working with the clients that live in the same community as you. Very good.

Speaker: I would say that in the community, somewhat like the institutions, we are intentional about everything that we do, every meeting that we have, every word that we say, every interaction, every piece of body language that we have. We aim to be very intentional with individuals, to have that impact and continue what was taught in the institution. I started in the institution and came back into the community, and now into training. It's just so big to be intentional and to want as much for that individual to change as they do.

Jane: Lovely. Thank you very much, Community Corrections for sharing your voice. Goodbye! I just want to stay here with Crystal and Joy. They have a sharp eye and were concentrating, and you may have noticed that they were both in three of the groupings. They are women, they work in the Department of Corrections, and they are in Community Corrections. I want to ask you, *Do you recognize those different, subcultural voices in yourself?*

Crystal: I do, specifically the last one. Being a probation officer has changed me the most, I think. Hearing how people are talking about the change in the clients that we work with. I worked at this institution for 10 years, so coming out here and seeing people interacting way differently than you would in an institution, that has changed me. And it has changed how I work, and how I view the Department of Corrections completely. It just opened up so many more opportunities to see that growth in both our clients and me as a person.

Jane: So that's the dominant subgroup voice in you now? Joy, what was your experience? Is it the same?

Joy: Yes. I did the majority of my time inside institutions, and I've done four years in the community. I think that exposure to both in the institution and the community has made me a better person overall because it puts all the pieces of the puzzle together. When you're sitting in one seat you can only see things from the seat that you're in. The Department gives us the opportunity to get different positions so you can see exactly how everything fits together. So I definitely follow Crystal that this exposure and experience within an institution and the community has made me a better individual. It has made me more knowledgeable about the whole process.

Jane: The more access you had to what I call those subcultural identities, the more experience you have, the more rounded you've become.

Joy: Yes!

Jane: Thank you both very much.

That was quite quick and enjoyable. A chance to see different subcultural groups. There are many, many more here. What I'd like to do if I had more time, is to put you into break-out groups, but we don't have time. Instead, I want to encourage you to think about it just for a minute, and to journal. Make a note of some of the subcultural groups that you are part of, and that are a part of you. We saw four of them. What are some of the groups that you are part of that are an important part of your life, and that show up a lot in you in this moment?

There is a second question that you can write down and answer later as your homework! What subcultural groupings do you see around you at work? Think about that overnight. I'm just going to finish with a couple of points and then hear the words written for us earlier in the chat. I'd like to save those to the end, just before our break.

What I'm saying is these subcultural identities are external groups, they're groups that you identify with, but they're also in you, a part of your identity and they come through you in what you think, say, and do. When you participate in a dialogue there's a part that is who you are individually, but there will also be subcultural voices that come through you. You probably noticed, for example, that the Virginia grouping may talk in a particular way or have a particular perspective in the Participatory Dialogues during this conference. Those voices come back more strongly if you are with people in your subcultural group. When I'm with women, my identity as a woman is much stronger than when I'm in a mixed-gender group, like here. When I'm with parents of kids who are a similar age to mine, that identity comes through much more strongly than when I'm not with them.

Another time that these strong subcultural group identities come through is if they are triggered by something. I may hear something on the news about parents needing to be more responsible for their children's use of social media, and I suddenly feel this kind of *whoosh* in me as I am triggered because of my views as a parent. Just a voice can trigger that in me.

Being part of these subcultural groups can have great benefits. I am not American, and I do not have a sorority, but I always thought it sounded like it might be a nice thing to have. A group of women that you're close with when you are at college. That can provide a nurturing sense of belonging. I hope in the Academy that we can do this, that we can be a subcultural grouping where we have common experiences and views, and we can support each other and give a sense of belonging.

Subcultural groups can also lead us to be defensive if we feel that our group is under attack. That means it can be a problem when there are conflicting storylines around you, and if those conflicting storylines are within yourself. We heard from some of the women who want to be committed to their job and committed to their family. Conflicting storylines internally can be difficult to resolve externally. You've got people who are parents saying they want more family-friendly work hours, and you've got entrepreneurs who are running the business saying, *No, I need you to be at work. I need you to be on call 24 hours a day.* You can of course get external conflicts between these subgroups.

So you will see when Harold picks up later today on the organizational level of Dialogue as Story, that these subgroup storylines are really important for organizational intervention and change. Do look out for them in the Participatory Dialogues that you go into later today and see what you discover.

Jane: In closing, I will read from the chat the words we missed because of the failing Wi-Fi:

Our culture is changing and women have become much stronger these days. Women are trying to make change every day and that means that they are creating a new story. We're trying to have more voice.

Beautiful words, and we're all behind you on that. Thank you.

Dialogue as Story: The Organization

Harold Clarke

Harold Clarke: Now we're going to talk about *Dialogue as Story* in organizations. You have heard Peter and Jane speak earlier on the *self* (or me individually) and then of *us* (as a group of individuals). You can appreciate that all the stories about *me* and about *us* are also present in organizations because people bring themselves when they come into an organization. All those stories are present. That makes it rather interesting to manage the diversity that is present in organizations, and that diversity impacts the culture of the organization.

I think we all understand that culture determines the degree to which an organization is successful. You can imagine what would happen if people came into an organization, where there is a vision and a mission, and a story line—but those individuals are not in keeping with the storyline. They're not in keeping with the vision and mission of the organization. You cannot expect the organization to be successful. Just as the culture influences success, the storyline influences the culture. As Peter Garrett once said, to change a culture, the storyline must be changed. The storyline must be addressed. You cannot have a storyline in your organization that has major deviations. Major deviations reflect fragmentation. Minor deviations are fine because minor deviations just reflect the diversity that exists, and diversity is welcome. Diversity is very powerful and can be very helpful. But when the stories, the many stories in the organization, divert significantly from the storyline then you have fragmentation.

Our Department, the Virginia Department of Corrections, is a very large Department. We are the largest state agency in the Commonwealth of Virginia. We are responsible for over a hundred thousand individuals. This includes inmates within institutions and supervisees who are on probation and parole in the community under our supervision and control. We also authorize 13,000 staff to supervise those individuals.

You can imagine the diversity that exists amongst the staff alone and the differences that they bring to the workplace that sometimes makes it a challenge to achieve our goals and our objective.

Therefore, we must be very deliberate about how we proceed within organizations. I mentioned that we are also training inmates within the organization in dialogue, in addition to the staff, because we believe that that is crucial. They are a part of the cultures in prison organizations, and to leave them out would be missing the opportunities to bring the entire organization together to be more successful. That fragmentation must be addressed. We can't ignore it. You must be deliberate and there are things that we can do within organizations to address the fragmentation. We must try to make sure that deviations from our storyline, which underpins everything, are addressed and that they're not pulling us away from our goals or objective.

Let me share some of my story in terms of what we did to deliberately change that which I viewed as fragmentation when I arrived in Virginia. We did things that we believe are making a difference today. A little later I'm going to have four of my colleagues speak to you as well, to give you an impression of the culture of this organization when they came in, and how things have shifted and changed over time. Of these individuals, Mr. Robinson has been here for over 40 years, Marcus Elam for about 30 years, Whitney Barton for about 10 years, then a gentleman who has only been with us for about three, Matthew Wibley. They are going to give you the chance to see, through their stories, how things shifted and how being deliberate can cause an organization to go in the direction you want it to go.

What did I see when I arrived in Virginia? My story, my observation, was one of fragmentation. The most obvious form of fragmentation was that we had two major divisions, community corrections and operations or prisons, that were very separate. They each had a deputy who responded to the director, but these two individuals did not engage with each other in terms of planning or thinking together in an effort to get the outcomes that we were seeking as an agency. They thought they were showing respect, one to the other, by not getting into the other person's business. Well, it was all of our business! One of the first obvious things we did was to combine those two major divisions—the community corrections and the prisons. We made several other changes to the structure of the organization to bring about the change. What I saw was a lack of trust. After restructuring staff meetings, people were not willing to talk because they did not trust each other. They didn't know what others were going to do with the information they shared openly in the meetings. As a result, people did not share much, especially when it came to decisions that they made that they could be held accountable for.

It was an organization in which safety and security were paramount. The focus was on safety and security, and they were not focused on cultural and developmental matters. Yes, there were some programs, but they were not paramount. The emphasis was on the safety and security of the organization. The leadership was top-down, *You do as I say!* A paramilitary organization. We had to do something deliberately. We could not just wish for a better organization. We could not just wish for change. We had to do something deliberate to cause change to occur. One of the things that we did was to introduce dialogue into the organization because I believed that with dialogue, everything else would fit. I always describe dialogue as a vessel into which you can place all your challenges and all of your opportunities and make sense of them together. We introduced dialogue throughout the organization, and we continue to do so. We introduced the concept of the Healing Environment to have people begin to think on healing in all senses, involving the inmates, the staff and the people with whom we interface in the community. We introduced Learning Teams and opportunities for others to get together and learn, using dialogue and we introduced several other business practices, including Working Dialogues.

Time is short so what I'd like to do is ask my colleagues to take about five minutes each to talk with you about when they came into the Department, what the storyline was, and what stories might give you an appreciation about the history of the agency and how we have moved on. Then we are going to get to the point when dialogue was introduced, and you'll see the storylines change from that point going forward. The first person I would like to call on is Mr. David Robinson. He's the Chief of Corrections Operations and has been with us now for over 40 years. David's going to tell you what things were like when he came in. What was the story? What were your experiences, David?

David Robinson: Thank you, Director Clarke. When I started in August 1982, we were a very small system. We had nine facilities that we would consider large today and those were scattered throughout the state. Mainly we had field-unit workcamps, and the purpose of those work camps was to send inmates out to do work out in the communities, on our farms, and with our Highway Department. We had about 2,500 to 3,000 staff, and very few of the security personnel or the correctional officers were women. We were not at all diverse regarding the number of women working in the ranks as correctional officers. Our leadership style was authoritarian, and it was very militaristic with regard to our chain of command. As the Director said, it was, *Do as I say, and you had better not ask why!*

The reality was that when the captain said, *Do it*, we pretty much did it. We had restricted communication. All of you are so used to cell phones and all this technology but we had no cell phones. Inmates didn't have phones—we had to dial the number for them. We didn't even have computers—we had typewriters. There was no cable TV, and there were no TVs for the inmate population. They just had am/fm radios. We had a real restrictive communication structure and very little programming. Our focus was not on rehabilitation or recidivism at all. It was focused on getting people out to work. Basically, our program was that we gave them $25 and a bus ticket, and we sent them home. We had a lot of lockdowns. We were having lockdowns everywhere. The theme, for me, was that we had no voice. We were in a state of real turmoil.

We had very few leaders that had vision or leadership. We went through four directors rapidly. Within the first two months of my career, I was involved in a serious fight where many people got hurt. The next day I thought, *Why in the world am I working here? I need to quit.* During the first four years of my career, we had hostage situations, we had riots, we had murders. There was no public trust in our system because we had the largest number of death row escapees in the United States of America. In reality, we were really out of control, with no leadership and a lot of violence.

Harold: I am the keeper of the time. Just hit the punchline!

Dave: Hit the punchline! OK. Today we have safety and control, but our emphasis is on recidivism and programs. We focus on creating lasting long-term public safety. The Director talked about oneness and how important that is. We're a national leader across the country, but we're still humble. We care and we're gracious about it. And we're a diverse organization from top to bottom. Everybody's voice matters and we delegate so as to stretch people to be the best they can be. And Dialogue, Oneness, the Healing Environment, and Learning Teams are our foundation.

Harold: Very good. Very good. Thank you. David. Next, we turn to Marcus Elam who has been with the Department for approximately 30 years. He came about 10 years after Mr. Robinson.

Marcus Elam: Thank you, Director, and good afternoon, everyone. The theme for me, when I started for the Department, would have been *us* versus *them*. The Director already mentioned this, and Mr. Robinson did too. I started off working in probation and parole in community corrections for my first couple of years. Then worked in an institution (prison) for a couple of years, another institution for a few years after that, and then went back to work in community corrections. I've been back and forth, in community corrections and institutions throughout my career. Early in my career that was pretty much unheard of and discouraged. What do I mean by that?

At that time, probation and parole did not talk to institutions. Institutions did not talk to folks in probation and parole even though we had a common theme of public safety and we all tried to provide services. There was no communication between the two divisions within operations at that time. It was even discouraged. I was a treatment program supervisor and we told counselors, *You don't call probation and parole*. If you had a question about an inmate and a release plan the people that investigated those plans at the time (and still do) are probation and parole, but a counselor could not call the probation officer to ask about a plan or try to do anything to help verify a plan. If there was a probation officer who received an inmate on release from the institution and had questions about any kind of programming experience that the inmate may have had while he was there, the probation officer was told, *You don't call the institution*.

Everybody had to call headquarters to get information. As Mr. Robinson mentioned, we didn't have computers back then. We didn't have any systems that could talk to each other. You literally had everything on paper, and you used carbon paper. You had to call someone at headquarters to get information about a prisoner. You could be working in Chesapeake probation, 20 minutes down the road from Indian Creek prison, and receive a released inmate but you couldn't call that prison or vice versa. Because there was no communication it really was detrimental to what we said we were about, which is public safety. Our leadership structure discouraged any real communication. The divisions were not connected at a lower level, only through the director.

We didn't share resources, and community corrections traditionally did not get funded for a lot of the resources that it needed. There was no talking to institutions or the regional director of institutions to try to get resources, whether it be equipment or dollars to be able to provide support for those folks who were on supervision. There was no sharing of resources and ultimately, as Mr. Robinson and the Director mentioned, there was no trust. We didn't know what the other was doing. We didn't talk to each other. We had no trust.

The other big thing during that time was that we didn't even meet. I was a Unit Head at that time, and I think we had one meeting a year where the wardens and the Chiefs got together—and we all sat at tables with the people that we worked with. We never associated with each other, and we never had conversations with each other. Other than that, we never met with a Warden. Community Chiefs never even knew who the Warden was. You couldn't get them on the phone, and they couldn't get a Chief on the phone.

The way the organization was structured and the way we communicated was literally and completely fragmented. We didn't track things and we did not have discussions about how effective we were as an agency in relation to long-term public safety. An inmate could be in restrictive housing for long periods of time and the first time that inmate came out of a confined space with restraints was when the person was dropped off at a probation office on release, after serving many years in confinement. So there was no real continuity of care from the institution to community corrections and that was really detrimental to the overall effectiveness of the agency.

Once the Director came my storyline would change to be true *oneness*. At his very first meeting in our training academy, he talked about dialogue, and he was very clear that as an agency we have to operate as one. That really forced me and other leaders at that time to really think about how we operated and how we were going to operate moving forward. We lost some people during that time. We had some folks that did not want to go through that type of change. They liked the way things were. It took a lot of learning. We became a learning organization. So my storyline now is that we are one, truly one. Our systems are connected and talk to each other. We do not meet without one or the other. Our unit heads from both divisions talk and meet routinely. There's constant communication, and I would say dialogue has been the vehicle for that.

Harold: All right. Well, thank you, Marcus. Let's give our attention now to Whitney Barton who has only been here for 10 years. So Whitney, what's your storyline?

Whitney Barton: Hi everyone. I'm glad to have this opportunity to share my story, my experience. I came into the agency, as Director Clarke said, about 10 years ago. The storyline or the theme at that point was re-entry and rehabilitation. I came in after the governor at that time had introduced the Virginia Adult Re-entry Initiative. Through that initiative, Director Clarke was appointed director. So he was already here and things were already in progress when I came into the agency. I knew the focus was rehabilitation and my previous career was as a social worker with the Department of Social Services, another state agency in Virginia. The drastic difference coming into the Department of Corrections was how large it was and how connected I felt, not only to where I was working but to the whole agency.

We went through training, and they talked about oneness in the training. I started as a counselor but in my training, there were people from the community, from probation and parole, from facilities all across the state. We were all there together, training. That was a huge difference for me. The other thing that stood out to me was that when I worked for the Department of Social Services I didn't know who the Commissioner was. I didn't know their name; I never had an expectation that I would meet that person and I never did interact with the Commissioner in the almost five years with that Department. So, I remember very clearly not long after I had been at the prison where I was working being called by the leadership and saying, *We need you to come up. You're going to talk with the director today.* I was like, *What? I'm going to talk with the director and the leadership. Really?* We were in a room together, seated in a circle, and they really wanted to hear what we had to say. They were asking us questions and really wanted to hear our voices. It was a culture shock for me coming from another agency— and that other agency was much smaller. That was less than a year after I started working in the Department of Corrections.

The opportunity was given to become a Dialogue Practitioner. I was immediately interested and wanted to jump right in because my background was in social work, helping people and rehabilitation. That is my passion. I jumped in, feet first, or head first, I don't know. I wanted to be a part of this. Being a part of that Dialogue Practitioner program allows you to see the entire agency through a different lens. You know that you're part of something bigger than your own work unit, you're part of something really huge. I've had the opportunity over the last 10 years to see that grow and develop, and the culture is even stronger now.

Harold: Thank you. Now we'll turn to Matthew Whibley who has been with the Department for three years. He just showed up and found out where the bathrooms were last week!

Matthew Whibley: Yes, thank you, Director, and good afternoon everyone. I am going to be sharing just one particular storyline I saw when I joined the agency in 2019. It was a story of dialogue entering its adolescence. The agency has made tremendous strides in implementing the changes that you just heard about from the other co-presenters. After about 10 years of dialogue at the Department of Corrections, the very fabric of the Department had been altered. Adolescence is an exciting time in an individual story. New questions, new identities and new challenges come out in a lot of new learning. The agency was learning some new things about dialogue and its practice of dialogue had been exceptional at addressing opportunities at the unit level. However, as we addressed more and more opportunities at the unit level, certain issues would arise during dialogues that were outside of the control of that individual unit. These issues were symptomatic of a complex government organization regulated by external agencies and accountable to elected officials and to the public.

We say dialogue works best when all the people who are needed to solve an issue are in the room but when the issue affects 12,000 employees and the solutions are influenced by external groups it can be really hard to find a room big enough to fit everybody. When I arrived the agency had recently implemented a series of annual dialogues that would take place at every unit. These dialogues all shared a similar common theme. Some of these issues came up, again and again, and we keep talking about it and nothing ever came of it. We never saw any results on this topic, despite it being shared in circles across the state. These experiences of shared frustrations within the complexity of an interdependent state-run organization formed part of one of the storylines prevalent at the time.

Deliberate action was taken by our leadership to address the voice of our staff, and this is where my work begins. It's a very intimate thing to work with the voice of staff, and it is almost more intimate to work with change. We are all a little bit apprehensive when it comes to change but at the same time, many of us yearn for it. My work entailed the careful and deliberate organization of employee comments from dialogues into an evidence-based framework for analysis. Over the course of three years, my team and I organized over 20,000 employee comments on topics like supervisor support, diversity, equity and inclusion and Covid-19 conditions. We were figuring out answers to questions like, *How do we make sense of complex issues happening all around the state* and, *How prevalent are these issues?* We developed a way to organize the information and to identify the major issues facing the entire agency.

With this process, we were able to provide an agenda to our leadership that enabled them to chart a course of deliberate action on the most important issues affecting the well-being of our staff. It also enabled us to return to our staff and show them in writing and policy and in action what we had accomplished with their input and their voice. It gave us an earnest response to the question, *What has come out of these dialogues?* And as we continue along this road of dialogic practice, the shared meaning and understanding generated in dialogues at the unit level are now interwoven into a shared storyline, allowing us to bridge the stories of individuals, units and regions into a story that makes up one Department of Corrections.

Harold: A good ending point—thank you, Matthew. And thank you all for your contributions this afternoon. Before I hand it to Jane, I want to make some closing comments. I hope that what sticks with you is the fact that *the culture drives the organization*. It's going to determine the success rate of the organization. In turn, *the storyline drives the culture* and the infrastructure. So, you must know your story and your underlying storylines. You must manage the story and the storylines. You must change the narrative if you intend to have a culture that is going to be responsive to the objectives and needs of the organization. As you can imagine, there are lots and lots of stories at all levels within an organization the size of ours. What I found to be the tool that served us best for all the changes structurally and otherwise that we put in place— the thing that was able to bring those together—was dialogue. That's why I always describe dialogue as a vessel into which I can place all our opportunities and all our problems to make sense of them together. Thank you all very much.

Jane Ball: That was a very, very compelling illustration of the development of the story and storylines in Virginia. A rich and fulfilling day, and again a lot to think about and sleep on.

Dialogue as Story: The World

William Isaacs

Dialogue and the story of now

Bill Isaacs: Some of us working on dialogue over many years have found a particular way of thinking helpful. We have said that the problem we face really isn't getting into a dialogue, but recognizing that the dialogue is already happening; the question one faces is, *How do you become aware of this, and learn to participate in it?*

When people first begin to explore this field, they tend to take a more individualized approach. They have the idea that when they enter a conversation, they should try to get people to talk together more effectively than they might otherwise. They try to apply techniques to give everyone space to speak, to remain open to new ideas, to relax their certainties. In doing so, it often becomes apparent that people are thinking in very different ways from each other, and they need to learn to listen more fully and without reaction or resistance. While this is helpful, it still oddly embodies a fragmentary view, one that says, *I'm here, you're there, and we're starting to connect better.*

In our conversation we are pointing to something else, something more subtle; the notion that there is a flow already moving in which we are all participating, but that we perhaps didn't notice. We didn't notice because we're often very involved in our own meaning-making. We're involved in our own reactions—to others, to what arises in ourselves, to our thinking and feeling. We typically think in terms of individuals as independent particles, not participants in a wider field of shared meaning. There is not necessarily anything wrong with this, and in some respects, it is certainly valid. But it can also lead us to miss what is going on beneath this. The challenge before us is to learn to participate in something larger than ourselves, the already existing flow or field of meaning and energy. Then questions arise, *How do I do that? What is that? How large is it? Where are its boundaries?* These questions lead to the theme I want to invite us to explore.

Take a look at this image. How large are you, really? Where do you stand in relation to the planet? I love this image because it invites you to step back and notice a much larger context, to become aware of the fact that we are actually embedded in the fabric of the planet, not separate from it.

The *story of the world*, as we are discussing it here, could also be called *the story of now,* the urgency of now—the moment now that we're all in. There are terms Marshall Ganz at Harvard introduced many years ago. As he points out, we all carry several different kinds of stories.

There are a number of dimensions to *the story of now* that we could point out. First, the global pandemic produced an unusual and novel condition, one where a large number of people around the world shared the same experience at the same time, while also being aware of this fact. This has never happened before. Certainly, in recent years, the interconnective tissue of the internet and various other modern communication processes have compressed us and brought us into a more shared space. Then the pandemic came, and we all had the very same set of factors to deal with—everybody, everywhere. This was truly unprecedented. I think that was a training opportunity for us—to come into an awareness of wholeness—a shared experience held in common by everyone.

Then a more intense shared experience arose when Russia invaded Ukraine. Without for the moment evaluating or taking sides about this situation, it is evident that the war intensified everyone's experience, and generated a great deal of polarization, disruption, and reaction. Not only did we now have a shared experience, we had a shared pattern of conflict and intensification, one with historical roots that many believed we had left behind. And because we're wired together so fully, we got (and still get) images of an intense war zone delivered daily on our phones. There's never been a circumstance where an event like this was so vividly thrust into our shared awareness.

These global challenges aren't really very far away from any of us anymore. This alone is an important element of the story of now. I would like to remind you of a few other factors and then ask you to reflect on your story of the larger challenge we all face, the *story of now* as you see it.

As everyone is aware, natural disasters are on the rise all around the planet. You don't have to be a big believer in climate change to notice that this is the case. While people still debate the causes of the climate that are emerging, the fact of them is undeniable.

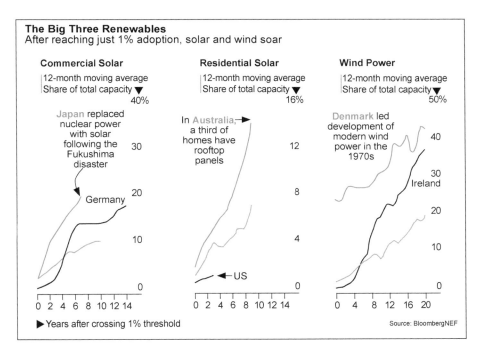

We are also in the midst of a rapidly intensifying global energy transition. This image shows how countries that decided to adopt some level of renewable energy saw this move from a small percentage of their total energy mix, 1% to 5%, to 30% to 40% over a very short period of time. At the same time, the price of renewables has come down much farther than anyone dreamed possible. We are in the midst of a gigantic set of changes here, ones that will have dramatic impacts on social and economic systems. There is also in many places a strengthening march towards right-wing authoritarian forms of government. This is evident in Israel, in the US, and in many countries in Europe. Populist energy is becoming more embedded and more central in governments now in a way that hasn't been present since the 1930's.

How do you see all of this? One frame is that these are a series of difficulties happening to me, and to us, with intensifying force. The framing we could however take is, that these things are not happening *to* us, but moving through us. Can we hold space for the greater intensity all of this represents? This is the challenge of dialogue—holding space for the larger flow, whether it involves people differing with one another in a room, or the intensities arising on the planet. Who can hold this? What is the story you have about this moment, and what is your responsibility towards all of this? This is the challenge I wish we would all pay attention to. I'm going to ask you to think quietly about all that for a few minutes. Then we will go into small groups, come back and have a conversation all together.

Let's begin by asking ourselves this question, *What is the larger challenge you wish we'd all face?* If you could have everyone really think about something that really mattered to you, what would it be? What would happen if we did that? What needs to change in you and in us for all this to occur? What's your vision of what would happen if we did that?

Break-out trios

Comments after the breakouts:

Bill: All right, welcome back. We have a few minutes to reflect on what you thought of this story of now, which is also the story of the world. What is our moment? What is this moment we're all in? How do you make sense of it? What do you think? What are you hearing? What are you feeling? Let's see if we can let flow happen among us for a few minutes.

Speaker: The way I answered the first part of the question was that everybody wants to be loved and be heard for who they are. The ways that I can help achieve this are to be transparent, to trust more of my voice and my truth, and to love more and accept people for who they are in their space.

Speaker: It is tempting to put your head in the sand because it's brutal watching the way this is playing out. But maybe what we need to do is reframe it. It has been framed as if everything is good and evil, not right and wrong. I can deal with right and wrong.

I can't deal with good and evil. Let's put our toe into the water and bring dialogue into these conversations. Maybe take the news in smaller doses so we can survive it, and then move into dialogue with the people with whom we agree and disagree.

Speaker: Our group spoke about homelessness, drug addiction, overdoses and wrongful convictions. We all become so desensitized and put our heads in the sand, but if we can utilize dialogue, I think it could be a great catalyst to help some of these issues that we're facing today.

Speaker: We talked about peace and our commitment to erasing homelessness and hunger and so on. What we wanted to change about ourselves is to embrace what's going on, to hold it, and yet not give up hope. Even if you're only doing micro-actions to build peace, never give up hope because change can come in any which way. And conflict is the other side of innovation.

Speaker: Homelessness and hunger were the focus of our group. If we could all live in a state of suspension, not judgment of one another, how would that look if we could all have that in common?

Speaker: We talked about global issues, the polarization of society and how we stop connecting with each other as a nation. When we are discussing political issues in a country, and we see each other as you against me and not as a single nation. What if everybody tries to have a dialogue based on a common goal, where the issue is my country and what we are going to solve as a nation? I'm not against you and you're not against me. How will the world look if that happens?

Speaker: Peace, climate change and education. And some agreement that education may help us to be more discerning in the information we are unwillingly being fed every day. What is fake information, and what is real information and news? Our confrontation comes from misunderstanding those things. It's my personal belief that education might help us to start solving those other aspects—getting to non-confrontation and reducing the difficulties with peace.

Speaker: I thought the third question was especially difficult. I was thinking about inequality in the world and the children that don't have enough food and have no shelter. What would I do? I would very much like to help that, but the question is how far out of my position of privilege am I willing to move to do that? Dialogue helps us understand those issues and have compassion for them. But it's taking the next step that gets really hard for me. If I want a dish of ice cream, I just go down to the store and get it. Am I willing to give up that privilege? That's what I'm struggling with.

Speaker: It seems like there are some common themes, homelessness and hunger. We added gun violence. The thing that we pinpointed is how society has become individualized and everyone is for assault. A lot of people need to start with *self*, by looking in the mirror and asking themselves what can I do to make a difference? We used to operate with the village mentality, where everyone helps someone. Now society has gotten to the point where everyone is looking out for themselves. Everyone seemed to have the same concerns overall.

Bill: I want to thank you all. There's a lovely phrase that you often use, Harold, about being in a healing environment. There are all sorts of things to do in an external sense, rules to follow and people to handle. That's true in every context. But producing an environment, an atmosphere in which healing is possible, despite some quite intense factors, seems to be a good example of what's needed. We have some experience about how the space of dialogue provides that. It's not always easy to articulate what difference it would make, but here we are considering how we might not be stuck in reaction to what's going on—and how we might be able to provide something different. That's significant, and an immediate contribution. That is by far the highest leverage thing—to do something about how we are in the world. There's taking the pollution out of the pipe when it comes out into the river, but there's doing something about what gets put into the pipe in the first place. Dialogue is about going upstream of all that. And that's very potent. Doing that changes the whole situation in ways you can't necessarily mentally figure out.

Speaker: An additional thanks, Bill, for your consideration through the time you have led us in this consideration. It is occurring to me that a battery has a positive or negative end, and if you put the battery the wrong way around, it doesn't work. Put it the right way around you and you have energy. There are a lot of people asking, *What will I get out of this?* Or saying, *I'll put something in if I am going to get something out of it.* But that's the wrong way around and the situation is very scrambled. I appreciate you bringing out the idea about how we place ourselves in the world. It's partly inclusion, and it's partly providing space for things to work out. I like your emphasis of this particular state whilst we are looking at the story across the world, across humanity. What is our role in that? I think you brought that out rather well. I appreciate your presence and your words in doing that, Bill.

PART TWO

THE ORIGINAL PAPER: DIALOGUE AS STORY

By Peter Garrett

Dialogue As Story

Preamble

Although it only coalesced in my thinking in early 2022, Dialogue as Story has been implicit in my practice of Dialogue since 1993. That is when I began a weekly Dialogue Group that ran continuously for some seven or eight years, with an average of 18 participants in a high-security prison. During that time, I noticed how the participating prisoners and staff members re-assessed things as they listened to each other. Their descriptions of themselves and their own lives shifted a little each time they revealed glimpses of their own experience. How they referred to each other changed, as did the way they talked about the situation in the prison where they lived or worked.

Looking back, I would now say that they were making sense of things by reviewing the stories they held – stories about themselves, the subcultural groupings of which they were a part, the prison and about society as a whole.

This sense-making has fascinated me ever since. Every day we have first-hand encounters, and we read and hear about things from others. I now realise that to make sense of what is coming to us from various disparate sources, a kind of story emerges in our thinking. We create a story about the situation to make meaningful sense of what we perceive, individually and collectively. This story-making is so automatic we hardly notice that it is going on all the time. It seems we are just observing things, but we seldom observe our own creation of story as we do so. These stories accumulate in memory and shape our perception and what we choose to notice about things that are happening now. In this way our many stories not only contain information about what is happening around us – they also reveal much about us the authors and our identity, disposition, intention and capability.

There are significant implications to recognising story as the form of our sense-making process . . .

Dialogue As Story

Peter Garrett

What is Dialogue?

The word *Dialogue* is derived from *dia* which means 'through', as a diameter is a line drawn through the centre of a circle, and *logos* which is 'the word' or 'meaning'. Dialogue, therefore, as it is used in the Academy of Professional Dialogue, is a way of talking and thinking together to find a common meaning through and amongst a group of people. This is important because when people do not hold a common understanding or meaning, the many decisions they make are disjointed and they inadvertently trip each other up through the actions they take. In the absence of a common context or meaning to guide decision-making, organisations often try to align people's actions through procedures and rules that are intended to guide and determine people's actions. Some organisations have a rule book as thick as an encyclopaedia and expend a significant amount of time and resources in training and enforcement to try to achieve compliance. It is not difficult to see that a different way of working that incorporated Dialogue could make a significant contribution to the smooth functioning of an organisation.

We make sense of things by generating stories

If we want to use Dialogue to find or generate a common meaning, then it would help to understand how meaning comes about. Meaning emerges from the way we make sense of the disparate things we encounter, and that we hear or read about. That sense-making takes the form of combining things into a kind of story. We might expect someone at a meeting and if they don't arrive at the anticipated time, we find ourselves with a story about why not. This is an automatic process that we hardly notice and cannot stop from happening. I see the wind blowing the trees, I hear a door bang shut, and I assume there may be a relationship between the two, and that the wind blew the door shut. The connecting story might be, *It was such a windy day that the wind even blew the door shut!* Or perhaps I hear two people arguing, followed by a door slamming shut, and the story that appears in my mind is, *It was quite an argument, because I heard one of them slam the door as they left*! It is natural to connect the things we see and hear. We need to do so to operate our daily lives. We form stories that connect things meaningfully to one another. We do it all the time without noticing that we are doing so. The assumptions involved in the story can seem so self-evident that they must be true. *I was there. Let me tell you what happened!* The stories are perhaps reinforced or modified by new observations or information, building story upon story into a broader meaning and understanding of the situation. Some aspects of our stories appear more significant, and we attach greater value to them, whilst other parts seem irrelevant to us, although not necessarily to others.

These sense-making stories combine the past, the present and the future

These accumulated stories have other features that are easily overlooked. The stories are about what has happened in the past. Without our noticing it, however, they continually inform what we observe. They influence our interpretation of the current situation and shape how we decide to act in the present. They also carry implications that lead us to anticipate that certain things are likely to happen in the future. *If the wind blew the door shut, perhaps I should close the windows . . .* ' or, *If they are having a serious disagreement, perhaps I should be quiet and keep out of sight . . .* In this way, stories connect the past with the present and the future. That is a peculiar achievement, because essentially the past is present through our memory, and the future is present through our anticipation based on projection or imagination. Although it does not seem to be that way, we are forever stuck in the present. I visited a bar/restaurant in Cape Town that understood this well. It had a never-claimed offer, flashing enticingly in neon lights, *Free beer served here tomorrow!*

Beneath the story there is a simpler storyline that holds the assumptions, logic and implications

This connection between the past, the present and the future contributes to the *storyline* that lies beneath the story or set of stories. Removing the details, it is the generic essence of the story. The storyline is the way in which the story develops, including its assumptions, logic and consequences. Storylines can become habitual and repeatedly applied in different circumstances, forming a general pattern. For example, speaking about their workplace, people might say, *In this organisation we never do things the easy way!* or, *It may take time, but we always get there in the end!* Another favourite is, *Nobody enjoys change.* Some storylines are re-used again and again in the myriad of short stories formed about the vignettes of daily life. Any good practitioner will recognise the repeated storylines that are an integral part of a culture. The storylines generally involve success or failure, joy or pain, luck or skill, misfortune or error. There are relatively few storylines, and they are repeatedly used in most books, plays and movies. The storyline of a comedy, for example, typically involves misunderstandings that surprise and confuse people in a way that turns out to be harmless (as in Charlie Chaplin movies), whereas the storyline of a tragedy involves misunderstandings that end in pain and suffering (as in the Shakespeare play *Romeo and Juliet*). There are individual storylines, and there are underlying and commonly held storylines in families, organisations, subcultural groupings, communities and nations. They bind people together in a common sense of success and failure by being replicated in the apparently logical outworking of endless incidents. They do not necessarily hold up to *factual* scrutiny, but they actively contribute to how people make sense of things.

To change the culture, you must change the storyline, or things will regress to what they were

This way of thinking about sense-making, story and storyline gives us an insight about how to change a culture. Leaders, and their advisors, often talk about the challenge of changing the culture of their organisation or community. It is seen as a difficult task because that culture can seem so pervasive and nebulous that it is not clear where to start. You cannot get your hands on it. Well, at the core of that culture, or subculture, are the relatively few collectively held storylines. They lie unnoticed, authoring the tone (and to some degree the content) of the description of the many incidents that occur every day. If you can recognise these storylines, and successfully intervene to generate new ones, then you will change the culture. On the other hand, if you make organisational and procedural changes without changing the primary storylines, things will quietly regress to their original state. That is the power of the storyline. It led to Peter Drucker's observation that *Culture eats strategy for breakfast*.

Sense-making stories reveal much about us, the authors of the stories

Our stories, embodying their underlying storyline, are a rich form of narrative. They convey far more than the *facts* contained in an apparently *objective* report. They describe more than is happening in the situation around us. In telling a story we reveal elements of what has value and significance to us, and the sense-making process we use in connecting things to one another. This is the wonderful thing about stories. As well as describing the key characters and the plot, we reveal essential elements about ourselves as authors and narrators. Through our stories we display our predisposition and how we feel about things. How we are disposed is a story about how we feel about the situation. Whether we mean to or not, we reveal our intention and what we are trying to do. It is the story of where we are headed. And we disclose how capable we are, the combination of our skill and capacity to do what we want to do. At a deeper level, we reveal who we experience ourselves to be. Our identity is not a label or role, it is a story with a storyline. If we lose touch with our storyline we falter, uncertain how to proceed. A loss of employment or home, a divorce or an incarceration may indicate a broken storyline.

Identity is not a thing, it is a story and has an underlying storyline . . .

These elements of *disposition, intention, capability and identity,* are inherent in any story. They are the very things that coaches seek to address individually with their clients, and that practitioners seek to address collectively within organisations. At an organisational level, the stories may vary in emphasis in different teams, departments or subcultural groupings, but they have a common source, which is the collective sense-making of the organisation. We start to see that the stories told every day across an organisation are not just descriptions – they are interpretations based on an underlying storyline. In total, they *are* the disposition, intention, capability and identity of the organisation. As Henry Ford apparently said, *Whether you think you can, or you think you can't, you're right.* It is one large, disjointed organisational story, variations of which are continually being told locally in every part of the organisation.

When is it diversity, and when is it fragmentation?

When people talk and think together, each participant is revealing parts of their story and what they believe about the situation and the circumstance. Although these stories may be about the same incidents and activities, they differ according to the author and the pockets of collective understanding they encounter. Naturally, there are differences between people and what they think, feel and say, since every individual is unique and has their own way of expressing themselves and their views. Sometimes these differences can be celebrated as diversity, at other times they are condemned as confusion. When the individual stories are differentiations of a commonly held storyline, then that is evidence of a healthy diversity – where different people are respected for their different ways of describing much the same inner experience. On the other hand, when the various stories are so disjointed that they share little in common, then we have fragmentation. They are not descriptions of the same thing, but stories with fundamentally different storylines. That fragmented state leads to conflict, which can escalate into violation and (in the extreme) into violence. The source of the violence is an attempt to *kill* the opposing storyline. This poses a dilemma. We may not be able to accept or accommodate a conflicting storyline but attempts to destroy it damage our own storyline. We need to find or generate an underlying sense of wholeness that can only come about through inclusion, not exclusion. Fragmentation cannot be transformed into diversity without changes in the conflictual storylines. Recognising these storylines, and enquiring into their origins and implications, leads us to see more generative interpretations.

Fragmentation originates in consciousness

If we take the time to ponder on it, we discover the obvious – that fragmentation originates in human consciousness. Things are interconnected everywhere, apart from in our conscious awareness. For example, there is only one earth, with an atmosphere whose state we describe in terms of the climate and the weather. Acting without this awareness, we can ignore the pollution we create and its impact causing the deterioration of the only atmosphere we have. The atmosphere is fully interconnected, hence the impact of pollution that drifts across human borders. It is our awareness that may be partial or fragmented, leading to disjointed action. Similarly, there is only one human race living on earth. Are our nations and communities expressions of enriching diversity? Or are there conflictual storylines for different nations and communities that display the consequences of fragmentation? Both are visible. We can recognise that both diversity and fragmentation are evident at different times and in different places. Another example is the economy. We can recognise that there is a single worldwide economy, with interlinked trade, currencies and banking systems. Yet, taking currency, each country may try to strengthen its currency without regard for the directly linked impact it has on weakening the exchange rate of other currencies. Things are inherently interconnected despite our disconnected stories.

Fragmentation is evident in form

There is a compounding problem. Fragmented human consciousness leads to actions that disrupt the inherent patterns of interconnection. The external fragmentation is more visible and concerning than the internal cause. That leads us to attend to the problem out there, rather than the source of the fragmentation that is in consciousness. This fragmentation in consciousness is deeply rooted in commonly held storylines. Nationality is one example. It is good to be proud of one's country and its contribution to human civilization. It is natural to celebrate when one's country is victorious in sport or receives awards for artistic or human endeavour. But along with that, there is a commonly accepted underlying storyline that is at the root of huge problems in the world. Patriotism says that our country comes first and must be defended to the point of death. Despite geographic, climatic, fiscal and social interdependence, we uphold the sovereign right of nations to make decisions independently of each other. Sovereignty has a storyline to it that does not respect the whole. It puts us and our nation before other nations. Humanity is an international identity that is also present, and engenders responsible diversity, but the sovereign right of each nation is far more deeply embedded. Sovereignty, held independently of humanity, confuses our disposition and intentions, what we can do and what we believe it is necessary to do. Clearly, we need to understand more about the roots of fragmentation in human consciousness.

Levels of fragmentation

The stories we tell (and hold) lead to our experience of the world and the experiences we have in our lives. Many are good enough for us to manage well. There are times, however, when things are not working out as we anticipated. Then, instead of reproducing our stories more forcefully (through playing our memory tapes more loudly) we need to check their validity. This requires that we think, and that we enquire. We need to check what we believe, or if what we are so convinced about that we *know* is indeed true. In our stories we may be putting things together that are not as directly related as we believe them to be, or we may not be relating things in our awareness that are more directly related to each other than we believe. The relatedness may have been valid when the stories were first formed, but things may have changed since then. A mother may see her son through childhood stories although he may now be a mature man in his 50s! A family may have been wealthy in the past, but circumstances may have changed and economising may be necessary.

This problem with the relevance and validity of the stories we hold in active memory occurs in various ways that we may easily overlook. The generic outcome is fragmentation. Indeed, the problem of our age is social fragmentation. There are deepening levels of fragmentation.

How I see it is how it is: The primary source is the deceptive experience that the reality I see is unaffected by and independent of my sense-making. That first level of fragmentation is summed up in the phrase, *How I see it is how it is*. That is true from one angle, of course, but how it is may be seen in a multitude of ways from many other perspectives. It seldom really feels that way. The more obvious feeling is, *I might be wrong, but I doubt it . . .* When we each recognise that what we say is a part of *our story* about how things are, then we make a step in the right direction.

A common content of consciousness: Perspective is one significant factor, but why else do people have different stories? The second level of fragmentation arises because we are not all aware of the same things. We have different information. We do not all have a *Common Content of Consciousness*. Some have experiences that others have not. We may have heard and read about things that have not been available to others. They may have had experiences that we were unaware of. The differing information available to the participants leads to different stories. On discovering new information that was previously lacking, one might exclaim, *Well, if I had known that, of course, I would have formed a different opinion and made a different decision!*

A localised mentality: A third level relates to parochial or narrowminded self-centredness. This involves a lack of feeling interconnected with the whole. It is a pre-occupation with one's own affairs, *In our team or organisation (community or country) we do it this way, and we are not too concerned how others do things*. It easily leads to an attitude of NIMBY (not in my back yard). Don't put your problems on me! Yet, how each of us acts affects others directly and indirectly. My cutting down trees leads to your lack of clean air. It is a single system, but my *localised mentality* leaves me unaware of that. Within a localised mentality it seems common sense to get on with one's own affairs and to look after one's own interests, as every populist politician knows. But through restricted scope, a localised mentality is anything but a common sense – it is an isolated sense, and it fosters fragmentation in an insidious way.

Interpretation: A further level of fragmentation is the assumptions I make, and the logic or rationale used in making sense of things. It is not uncommon for people to be present at the same event and to interpret what happened quite differently. That is why we have enquiries or investigations. We have *different interpretations* of what happened. Rather than debating who was right and who was wrong, it becomes more productive to explore why my story is different from your story. In this way, we are not essentially disagreeing with each other. Instead, we are exploring why our stories are different. Understanding another person's story requires attention, listening and respect. Understanding one's own story, and why one holds it as valid and true, requires suspension (the act of enquiring into your story as you describe it to others).

Subcultural thought: Thought is rarely held individually. Memory is largely a collective process where our stories or interpretations are shaped and reinforced by those with whom we associate. The most obvious form of this is subcultural groupings. A subculture is self-reinforcing because the validity of the views held is confirmed by those in the subculture who hold similar views. This can easily lead to erroneous and outdated stories that are still informing the thinking, disposition and actions of those in the subcultural group. These memories are reinforced by the emotions present at the time the story was formed, making them difficult to shift. This is the root of much of the social and organisational fragmentation in the world. Shifting the storylines of subcultural groupings requires particular skills to counter collective regressing.

Putting Dialogue as Story into action

We have been considering the theory behind Dialogue as Story. Next is putting this into practice. How do we use *Dialogue as Story* to become aware of our sense-making, and to enhance our sense-making skills? The primary interest is not the noble art of storytelling. That is a form of monologue. With *Dialogue as Story*, we are exploring how story emerges through a group of people talking and thinking together. Typically, the Dialogue starts with a question so that people are actively enquiring. Even when they advocate a view in the Dialogue, they are encouraged to do so in an enquiring way – checking why they hold it and thereby deepening or changing its meaning. At the outset, the participants may hold different attitudes and positions about the question being considered, and they may agree or disagree with one another. *Dialogue as Story* is looking for something beyond that kind of exchange of opinions. It is an exploration into what happens when the participants give attention to the collective voice – rather than hearing the individual voices as distinct from one another and caused by the interactions between different individuals. Usually, people listen to some speakers more than others, and want to exchange views with those they find more interesting. From the perspective of *Dialogue as Story*, participants are instead asked to listen to what is being said by every person, and to hear their words as a contribution to the collective voice of the group, as if the group was telling a single story. Rather than addressing other individuals, each speaker deliberately speaks to the whole group and listens to the whole group expressing itself. Each individual participates by considering what is happening in the room and enhances the collective story by contributing the story that is emerging from within their own thoughts and feelings. In this way, a new understanding is generated together.

Bystanding, suspension and proprioception

There is a sequence of awareness skills needed to put *Dialogue as Story* into action well. The first is *bystanding*, which is one of the four Dialogic Actions. Whilst most people easily understand *moving, following and opposing*, fewer are comfortable with *bystanding*. They wonder what it is, how to do it and why. Bystanding is stating one's observations about what has been happening. Not assessing or judging, but stating the sequence of activity that occurred. It is not a matter of simply repeating what was said – that would give evidence of competent listening. It is the skill that enables you to precis what has been said – to abstract the three key points made in the last half hour of conversation or Dialogue – and to say why noticing them is relevant. The practitioner who cannot bystand will have pages of notes, not a few key points. A good bystand will reveal the storyline underlying the detail of the conversation or dialogue – making available to everyone what has been influencing the thinking and feelings in the room.

Whilst bystanding involves reflecting about the past, there is a more immediate awareness-based skill called *suspension*. Suspension is the act of enquiring into your story as you describe it to others. This is less reflective and more immediate. Whilst still speaking, the speaker might notice the potential assumptions they have made, the logic they have used, how they reached a conclusion if they did, and the general validity of the view or opinion. Suspension, then, is holding one's story loosely for enquiry into its relevance and validity. An alternative meaning of suspension is to stop (like being suspended from going to school) but that is <u>not</u> what is meant here. Suspending a story helps to reveal the sense-making process in use. Suspension is the key to entering Dialogue. Collectively suspending views together takes the group directly into a dialogical enquiry.

As people become skillful at suspension, they may find their views are confirmed, or they may be less certain about their validity. They may see evidence of fragmentation in their sense-making. Indeed, they may find themselves in the unusual position of disagreeing with themselves! Agreeing and disagreeing with oneself is part of a process where memories are refreshed and updated. Being aware of what is happening as it happens may be called *proprioceptive awareness*. This is crucial because it enables adjustments to occur live in the moment, rather than through later reflection. *Proprioception* is the means of addressing fragmentation in consciousness. Collective proprioception is the aim of Dialogue as Story.

Incorporating all the stories in a common story is a form of Generative Dialogue

If we experience Dialogue as Story, we recognise that everyone plays a part in the collective story. For this to be the experience, we will need to discover and recognise the many different storylines at play, and to participate in generating a new story that incorporates them into a common story. This is a form of Generative Dialogue. Generative Dialogue creates different outcomes.

Peter Garrett September 2022

PART THREE

Participatory Dialogues Co-facilitated by
Members of the Academy

Section One

Participatory Dialogues: Me (The Self)

The core concept of Dialogue as Story is that we make sense of things in the form of a story. At an individual level, we each have an implicit story about ourselves, based on our many experiences, that is our identity. Four of the Participatory Dialogues explored this core story in some depth.

Tzofnat Peleg-Baker *and co-facilitator* **Justin Wooten** *explored the proposal that we would make better sense of ourselves if we not only included the parts of ourselves that we like but also stopped trying to exclude the parts that we do not. Accepting more of ourselves may reveal a vulnerable story of continually becoming, and through that a stronger connection with others.*

Bernhard Holtrop *similarly considered dual aspects to the individual story of identity, by seeing oneself as both a victim and an offender. Many participants in the Dialogue were from the same organization and explored this question in the context of their workplace Healing Environment initiative. Bernhard sensed this was valuable, and that participants were also avoiding a more personal exploration.*

Amber Leake *and* **Emilie Sattie** *considered situations where an act of violent crime had abruptly led to separate victim and offender identities. The damaged story can often go deeper and break the underlying storyline of an individual's self-identity. Victims may lose their voice, due to unanswerable questions, and become unable to author their ongoing identity story. Similarly, the perpetrator's story becomes stuck unless accountability is accepted. Sharing stories between victim and perpetrator is often deeply humanizing and healing.*

Elisabeth Razesberger *and* **Tzofnat Peleg-Baker** *asked, What makes us who we are? and, What situations make us aware of our identity? In this Participatory Dialogue, it seems that participants were self-aware and reflective — and they went deeply into their own experiences of what divides and fragments. They could see how their dark side impacts how they relate to each other, and how authentic stories can address stigmatisation.*

How Does Our Inner Dialogue, with Our Many Identities, Shape Our Outer Dialogue with Others?

Tzofnat Peleg-Baker and Justin Wooten

Pre-Conference Description

Understanding the self as multidimensional and evolving continuously through interactions significantly challenges the traditional conception of a bounded and fixed self of a person who constantly and effortfully protects self-perfection and coherence. The self, as a whole, embodies both the negative and positive, and a full range of dimensions (values, beliefs, and opinions) that sometimes contradict one another.

Negative dimensions refer to what a person does not accept within the self, like flaws, ambiguities, or inconsistencies. In contrast, positive dimensions entail what a person accepts within oneself, like what is desired or positively perceived by others.

Understanding ourselves as multidimensional beings rather than perfect, emancipates us from the burden of always being coherent and consistent. It normalizes our state of complexity and opens the door to empathizing with the complexity of others. We connect more dialogically through our grey areas, uncertainties, mistakes or incoherence. The Whole self is constantly in the state of becoming rather than being fixed. In this workshop, we will explore the idea of the extent to which our inner dialogue with our manifold self powerfully shapes our outer dialogue with others.

CHECK-OUT

Tzofnat: Before we wrap it up, the question that I would like us to say something about is, *So, how do we become friends with our multiple self?* To be more flexible with others, to connect with others in better ways, and to be more authentic. *What is one thing we can do differently to embrace this multiplicity?*

Speaker: We can recognize our annoyance and research it. See what is present in myself.

Speaker: If this happens to me again, I'm going to write it down and then I'm going to work on it.

Speaker: I have more of a curiosity around establishing permission within a dialogue or a group, to bring a voice and to name the annoyance and explore it together.

Speaker: I would say that we have to develop more dialogical approaches, including nonverbal dialogue —in the sense that sometimes you don't want to talk to somebody or perhaps because there's something burning inside you and speaking out might result in chaos. So, you can develop nonverbal dialogue. Just shut your mouth and allow the moment to take its course. In that way you'll be able to balance the moment with your own self. Things will go better rather than if you are not trying to be perfect at it. You can be present, verbally or nonverbally. Some situations might need you to approach it verbally and in some situations you might want to approach things nonverbally.

Speaker: With my kids, I'm getting them to learn conflict resolution amongst themselves. Three girls and then a younger boy. The girls are all pre-teenage. My pastor said years ago, about marriage conflict, *You two are a unit, so if you win and he loses, then you both lose.* So, if you are not feeling your best self, like you're upset, sometimes it's best to be quiet in the moment. Maybe tensions are getting high and for some reason we're not hearing each other. We're saying the same thing but the other person's still not getting it. Sometimes it's best to say, *Why am I getting so wound up about this thing? What is it that's triggering this than me?* Sometimes just being quiet, tabling it or writing it down and coming back to it later ends up making the situation better in the long run.

Justin: It's a pleasure to be part of this dialogue today and to co-facilitate. I really enjoyed hearing everyone's feedback.

Tzofnat: Great. Thank you so much and enjoy the conference!

POSTSCRIPT

What was intended?

This workshop aimed to explore the idea of an alternative way of perceiving oneself as opposed to a traditional way of perceiving oneself as well as to what extent different ways of perceiving ourselves shape the quality of our interactions with others. In other words, the idea was to investigate our inner dialogue about ourselves and how this inner dialogue shapes the quality of our outer dialogues.

What happened?

To trigger thought, the workshop began with introducing the implications of a conventional outlook, dominated by modernist Western individualist values on the prevalent perception of the self, other and how we relate to one another. A few divisive implications were presented, including a bounded, ideally internally integrated self, rational and coherent, constantly seeking approval and existing in a protective mode to defend a positive self-image; and another aspect who becomes secondary and peripheral in the shadow of the self, and consequently lead to distorted relational structure and destructive conflicts.

The consequence of defensive reactions to differences and disagreements and binary thinking of black/white, right/wrong, truth/false, and good/bad was also discussed.

By sharing the Yin and Yang framework, the complex self was introduced to show the positive/visible/acceptable parts of self and the negative/invisible/unacceptable parts, that we do not see or that we ignore, and that drive our actions and generate negative defensive habitual patterns. I used an exercise that demonstrated how we tend to react negatively to some people who trigger us and why. We discussed a few questions I proposed why we react negatively, considering the Yin and Yang framework and how we can redirect our defenses and transform them into learning experiences.

This led to a conversation about the alternative perception of the self as a *Whole* multidimensional and evolving instead of fixed and bounded – and how it keeps changing through interactions. The idea was to make the invisible parts visible and, by so doing, to emancipate the self from being trapped by (or conditioned by) invisible forces that hold us back, make us inflexible and stand in the way of expanding the mind, learning, and having a genuine dialogue. Recognizing the *Whole* multidimensional self supports the state of becoming through relationships.

Participants shared that they will use what triggers them as an opportunity to learn more about themselves (*write it down and then I'm going to work on it*): *Bring a voice, name the annoyance, and explore an annoyance together.*

What did I learn?

It is a complex topic and takes longer than 90 minutes to explore and practice.

No Healing, No Development

Bernhard Holtrop

Pre-Conference Description

I'd like to have an explorative dialogue about dialogue, healing and developing ourselves.

I walk this world with the idea that I, as all human beings, have an offender and a victim in myself. For both of them, in me, I hold the principle that healing is an essential part of developing myself.

'No healing, No development'.

How can dialogue contribute to our healing?

Some questions I'd like to explore around this:

- *What healing experiences do we have with dialogue?*
- *What preconditions do we need to create a healing space with dialogue?*
- *What principles would help us?*
- *How do you experience the interaction between your outer dialogue and your inner dialogue in this process?*

CHECK-OUT

Bernhard: What resonated in you that you will take with you out of this circle? Who would like to start?

Speaker: We have been using the word *healing* a lot. I believe that people have different connotations of healing and what it is to heal. We have a *healing environment initiative* within our Department. I introduced it many years ago and allowed people to do what they wanted to do with it. They played with it, they changed it and they made it what they wanted. But I think we still have the same storyline and that's what's keeping us together around the healing environment concept. Although we have variations, we still have the same storyline, and we have diversity. When I think of the healing environment, it means every and any opportunity to help make a difference, or to improve any situation or condition. When we speak about the healing environment, we speak about it in terms of the inmates, the probationers, and our staff as well. Because staff show up with baggage to work every day their very presence can cause us not to be successful at what we're trying to do. They have healing they need to address also.

Speaker: What I'm leaving with is the power of modeling. My colleagues have been a real inspiration with that. Coming alongside somebody in a dark moment, getting on your knees and really letting that person know, *I hear you. I'm beside you.* Let's look at a different way to do this. I also love what was just said, *What's the next opportunity, with either our words or our presence, to bring healing to the group that we're in?* So, modeling the way, and also acceptance. We can't always change the outcome, but we can manage our own acceptance of what is and isn't possible.

Speaker: I think inclusion is just as important as modeling because we want to ensure that everybody feels like they belong and are accepted. We all bring different things to the table, and diversity is important because everybody can add to the pot. I call it *gumbo* because I'm from south of Louisiana where we make gumbo and everybody brings something to have a delicious meal. I think if we allow everyone to bring their best and be included, we will be successful in every aspect of our lives, personally and professionally.

Speaker: It's very much about being oneself, daring to be oneself and speaking up from what is inside us. I have the impression that although we are in different parts of the world, we are following a similar track with dialogue. We follow similar principles and ideas and I think this is a great thing.

Speaker: I think people want to be appreciated and to have a sense of belonging. Through dialogue we show authentic appreciation, we listen, we engage and that helps the process.

Speaker: Make sure that you fully engage the person, not only through eye contact and talking to them but also with your body language. I tend to speak a lot with my body and sometimes, if I'm frustrated, I need to be more aware of it. Your expectations might be different from mine and sometimes you have to put that on the table, to agree to disagree.

Speaker: This whole time I have been stuck on the *give space, take space* principle. I think that's what's resonated with me. People do bring their baggage to work. It's impossible to completely remove your personal life when you come to work. The principle of *giving space* and *taking space* means that we're allowing people to process through things that might be happening outside of work because it does contribute to who we are as people at work. That's what I'm taking away. Allowing people space but also taking some of that space myself and reflecting and making sure that I'm coming to the table the best that I can, and being the best person that I can be.

Speaker: I really appreciate the reminder that facilitating anything for anybody is about leadership, and leadership is not dictatorship. When a dictator's running the show it's all about credit for them and only them but when a leader is leading the way everybody wins.

Speaker: I'm going to have realistic expectations and give myself the grace that I give to others.

Bernhard: Thank you everyone.

POSTSCRIPT

For this dialogue, I invited people to hold the principle that healing is an essential part of developing ourselves as individual human beings and as such contributes to the basis of developing organisations and society. I also invited the participants to have an exploratory dialogue about healing and developing ourselves and to see what dialogic principles may contribute to that. My intention was to create space for an open and vulnerable exploration about dialogue and healing, to share stories about our healing experiences, to learn from that together and to see what preconditions we could derive from that for creating a healing space.

Our online circle consisted mainly of participants from one organisation, which I realise played a role in how the dialogue unfolded. I experienced an open, positive, explorative, but mostly observational dialogue. The focus was on the organisation and on how to create and foster a healing climate there. People felt less inclined to share stories about their personal healing experiences. Out of this nice dialogue a wonderful, shared VADOC storyline emerged. One with a set of underlying values that were consciously embraced with gratitude. Participants said they realised they share a unique front-running working environment. The participants were inspired by each other's contributions and built further on them, sometimes bringing in diverting associations that could be integrated later on, thereby enriching the dialogue. The shared working environment seemed to contribute to the ease of bringing it all together and to help a storyline of values emerge. On the other hand, it probably also kept the dialogue more safe and less vulnerable. Less wow!

This brought up a double feeling in me. On the one side, it is great to be so happy together. On the other side was a hint of, *Is this it?* I was longing to learn more from the people I engaged with – to meet each other in vulnerability. I felt inclined to model this from my side and was met with sincere resonance, but the reservedness remained. This led me to realise limitations in the bandwidth of what was safe to explore for this group, online and in a relatively short dialogic setting. So, in the short time given together I chose to go along with the happy tone. If it had been a two-day outdoor session, in which we would have had more *trust-time*, I think more would have come out. And I certainly would have shown more curiosity and shared my intuitions more.

What I experienced positively was how this dialogue strengthened the narrative and underlying values of VADOC. It was attuning in a professional, loving way. Later, reflecting on it, I also noticed that compulsory vaccination for the staff lingered in the back of my mind. I can understand a dilemma for an organisation that adheres so strongly to open dialogue yet must follow a quite conflicting narrative from outside sources.

Violent Crime Changes People: How Does One Journey from Harm to Healing?

Amber Leake and Emily Sattie

Pre-Conference Description

When violent crime happens, victims are left to endure significant physical, financial, emotional, and spiritual impacts. These impacts may be acute or chronic and often influence other facets of a victim's life, like their work, relationships, or community.

Victims lose their voices quickly in the criminal justice system and often spend years dealing with unanswered questions and residual impacts from the abrupt change that crime had on their lives. Through the VADOC's Victim Offender Dialogue Program, crime victims have the opportunity to dialogue directly with their perpetrators. This interaction allows the victims to have their voices heard, express the impacts of the crime and put questions directly to the person responsible. It allows perpetrators to take responsibility and accountability for the harm they caused to others. This interaction is often life-changing for both parties and allows for a level of healing on both sides of a violent crime.

CHECK-OUT

Amber: We've explored a lot together today. The question that we started with was that violent crime changes people and we asked, *How does one journey from harm to healing?* We started with the victim survivor's perspective and then we moved into the inmate accountability perspective. We then had a period of talking together about sharing information or resources, helping people grow and helping people to find those resources.

My check-out question for you all is, *Having explored things together today for the last 60 plus minutes, what are you leaving with? Has your perspective changed?* Anybody want to volunteer to start?

Speaker: I've been quiet the whole time simply because I was leaving space for others. A lot of things I wanted to say were also already said, so I didn't want to repeat myself. But the main thing I'm taking away is that the victim has a right to their process and their process is the most important piece in recovery. I think that as long as we're focusing on that in the Department, I think we will heal the most and reach the people that we're supposed to reach when it comes to victims.

Speaker: As a survivor, it was helpful for me, as a reminder, to listen to some other survivors. Even though we all know this, sometimes we tend to forget that everybody's journey is different. Everybody's process is different. There's no right or wrong. It served as a reminder to me that sometimes I view friends who have never been a victim or a survivor a little differently because they say they understand but there's no way they could understand. I can't totally understand the experience of the other victims and survivors who spoke today. I can relate to certain things, but it re-emphasizes for me the uniqueness that we all have as survivors and how we heal.

Speaker: One of my takeaways from today is that the healing process is going to happen in different stages. First, there's the immediate reaction to whatever the crime was that happened to you. Then, if the perpetrator is on the loose and they haven't captured them yet, there's a stage where you're waiting for them to be captured. Then the court stage and, lastly, the processing or sentencing stage. The victims are thinking maybe they didn't get enough time for what happened, and of course, if it's for murder you're never going to get enough time to bring your loved one back. Then, after they served that time, there is the release. Now you've got to go through this stage of healing for the release—and how are you going to deal with that? And if you see the perpetrator out in the streets later on, how are you going to deal with that? So that's my takeaway, that the healing is going to take a lot of different stages. It's going to be a lot of different ups and downs. One of the most profound things I heard was that your goal is not to get back to who you were because you are not going to get back to who you were. The crime has changed you. Try to heal as best as possible for the person that you are now.

Speaker: Getting people involved, you find there are a lot of different perspectives and they're all important. I think that we need to keep in mind that everyone is an individual. They'll react and respond differently based on whatever criteria move them. So, we need to be open-minded.

Speaker: I would just say that moving from hurting to healing, it's a process. No one can really tell you when you should move or how you should move. It is a process. And one thing I think is that it is important to know your way or to learn your way to get to the next part of the process. Trying not to get stuck but to somehow know your way. Learn your way in order to move to the next step of your healing. But it is a different process for everyone. The journey is different for each one.

Speaker: My takeaway is similar. The journey from harming to healing is a process that is unique to each and every person that is involved. Whether a victim, a perpetrator, a family member or anyone else, it is unique to that person. For us to support others and for the person that's experiencing it we must become aware of what our story is. It's so connected in my mind to the theme of the conference and what we have all experienced in this session. We must be willing to take the time to understand the stories from everyone involved. That is what has touched everyone.

Speaker: I follow that it is a process both for the victim as well as the perpetrator. I think it's important that both heal. I think they need to see each other, to humanize each other, because I think both parties dehumanize the other to rationalize the crime that happened. Before healing can happen they need to see through each other's eyes how the crime affected both parties.

Speaker: Having been in this business for almost 38 years, the first 16 years working with victims and helping them tell their story to heal and move to some sort of recovery and to a reassertion of self—and then the last 22 with perpetrators that were inmates and probationers, the biggest thing that was reinforced and impacted my perspective today is the fact that the more I know, the more I need to know. I have learned so much from everybody in this dialogue. It reinforces the importance of story and the importance of dialogue, and how dialogue permeates through so many different situations to change the story.

Speaker: I'm following everyone, every detail. When someone said something, it was like I was going to say that. But one thing that I would add is that we have a lot of work to do, and a lot of work has been done. I think the Department is going in the right direction and I see that we will reach the victims as well as the perpetrators. We do have work to do, but we are on the road to success.

Speaker: We talk about both sides of this—victim and perpetrator. I think the big picture for me is about what we are doing to live up to being in the business of helping people to be better. When we do this correctly, we really contribute a great deal to long-term public safety.

Speaker: Being inside the institution, from the inmate standpoint, there is a need for inmates to hold themselves accountable for the actual crime they have committed and the effects they have had on others.

Speaker: For me, there are a lot of takeaways. Firstly, thinking about it in terms of stories from the victim's perspective and making sure that they have an opportunity to tell their own story. I think a lot of times their voices are taken away by the way the criminal justice system is set up. It's important to allow them to tell us their story, and to tell us what they need, rather than us determining what that is for them. Secondly, from the perpetrator's side, it is about figuring out how we weave accountability into their story. I don't think there's any way to move forward without that. They'll continue to justify and excuse themselves, and so we need to find a way to weave accountability into the story that they are telling so that they can truly do things differently and contribute to public safety rather than taking away from it. Thirdly. when I think of us as corrections professionals and about our story, I now see that we can't grow weary of doing the right thing. I think that's so important. A simple statement but so profound. It is something to keep in mind as we continually see these same issues. We can't grow weary of continuing to push forward, and we need to celebrate the small victories we do see.

Speaker: I follow a lot of what you said but I was reminded at the beginning of this discussion how, even though we've come a long way, it's still challenging for people to find resources to get help. It's a reminder to continue to push, to get information out there and to help. It's easy to forget things like that happen. The dialogue was a great opportunity to remind me of what Victim Services do and how important their unit is to the Department of Corrections, to help with healing on both sides.

Speaker: *Each one, teach one*, was what came to my mind. Each one, teach one, be that from the offender's side or the victim's side. Each one, teach one. That will bring in accountability and humanization.

Amber: As simple as it may sound, I think it is about challenging mindsets at all times. When you hear people say things, challenge it! I think the mind is a powerful thing and thoughts are very powerful. If you can change them or have someone think about how they're thinking and acting it can definitely produce a lot.

Speaker: My biggest takeaway is the importance of the victim in a dialogue. I think it gives victims the opportunity to express to offenders how they're feeling, how it made them feel and the impact of the crime on them. It also gives the offender the opportunity to try to understand how he affected the victim and the family members, and everyone involved. Also, I think it's important that the offender acknowledges his crime, or what it is that he did, and that doing so could help him to heal better. Having the victim speak directly also helps them heal. At first, I thought if I was offended by somebody, I wouldn't want to speak with them. I'd probably want to kill them or something! But I guess expressing how you feel is the first step to healing.

Speaker: Everyone is on a journey. I have to decide if I'm going to help them move forward, or if I'm going to hold them back through my interactions with them.

Speaker: My biggest takeaway is the victim and offender dialogue. We talked about healing as a journey, and if the journey can end in such a beautiful story as was told between the victim and the offender then we know that the work is being done. It's a stamp on all the efforts from both sides. I heard about the persona that we can create in the midst of the hurt and it seems that if you can get to the end of the journey through a dialogue between the victim and the offender the walls come down and you see just a person. You no longer feel like you're victimized or that this person is a bad person, and this is what he's done. It's like you're looking at two different souls. I thought that story was so beautiful and impactful, the story of the dialogue between the victim and the offender.

Speaker: I too am going to take away the Victim-Offender Dialogue. I've always been interested in that program, and I have a better understanding now that I've heard what people have gone through often of how important this process is. Not everybody heals in the same way but if we can assist one victim to heal through the process then I think that's a success for the Department of Corrections. I will take away what was said by someone at the end of the dialogue, *I'm not afraid of you*. Not only did she acknowledge that the perpetrator was going to be living in the same area—which a lot of times victims are scared about—but at the end she also said, *Maybe I can help you to find a job*. So that, right there, showed that she had started the healing process.

Amber: All right, I think I'll wrap it up. I also agree that we can't grow weary of always doing the right thing, like challenging mindsets and sharing experiences. A lot of what I've heard is that you are having crucial conversations on a regular basis with perpetrators. Whether they've committed a crime or not, we've all harmed someone at some point in our lives in some way, shape or form. Acknowledging that harm so we can move forward is critical for our own personal growth. Finding common ground and just moving forward. I love the idea of not just talking at each other but talking together with each other, and I love bringing the whole theme that *Dialogue is Story* into it and being able to show you guys a full circle from where we started with our Victim-Offender Dialogue to where we ended, and how impactful talking together and sharing these crucial conversations are. It is having a positive impact not only on victims and the community but also on our incarcerated and our community supervision population. I really want to thank you for participating and I hope that you continue to share your experience.

POSTSCRIPT

The intention for our participatory dialogue was to share the benefits and *magic* of the VADOC Victim Offender Dialogue Program. We wanted to highlight how individuals can find common ground by talking and thinking together despite an unusual circumstance where the topic is one of violent crime and the participants in the dialogue are the perpetrator and their victim. What we found was that for participants, victimization is a taboo topic and one where too many people are affected and not enough people have addressed, openly discussed or sought help for that victimization.

The Participatory Dialogue became an opportunity for participants to learn about the Program and then share their own experiences in a public forum. Participants supported one another in their shared trauma and openly discussed topics that hold deep emotional and personal meaning to them. For many, life is just too busy to slow down and dive into their story of trauma, whether too painful or for fear of judgment or a myriad of different reasons, and they do not realize how much that suppression is holding them back from moving forward.

Victims who participate in a Victim Offender Dialogue often describe afterwards how a weight that they felt for so long has been lifted from their shoulders. They did not realize just how much the emotions, the trauma and the unanswered questions were weighing on their soul. Preparing for and then sitting down to face the person responsible for those emotions and trauma, and having their questions answered allowed them the freedom to move forward with their healing. For perpetrators, the dialogue allows an opportunity to take responsibility and accountability for the harm they caused and to show remorse to the person most affected by their actions.

What Makes Us Who We Are?
What Situations Make Us Aware of Our Identity?

Elisabeth Razesberger and Tzofnat Peleg-Baker

Pre-Conference Description

This dialogue will create space to have an exchange about how we think our identity impacts the way we engage with others. We will think together about the parts of ourselves that make us who we are, and that influence how we approach life experiences.

Which parts are non-negotiable?
Which parts can we alter without losing ourselves?

In this dialogue we will hear from each other how we feel when our identity is challenged.

Are we able to deal with difference?
Are there common patterns emerging from difference?
How do we feel listening to people whose life is very different from our own?

CHECK-OUT

Elisabeth: Let's have a closing round, a check-out, to share a few thoughts about the session itself, and maybe what you're taking away. You could also share a new question that arose while listening to the others. It will not be answered today but might be in another dialogue.

Speaker: The question I'm taking away is how do we keep, through our own being, being unifiers constantly unifying differences?

Speaker: It is very important that we are carriers of dialogue, or natural facilitators, not just in groups but wherever we go. Let's not underestimate the power of social networks to divide us and keep us in bubbles of like-minded people, learning to hate those who are not in our bubble. Social networking is an incredible force and I hope many of us will go against that force because it's creating a new culture of enemies. I bring hope with me that as we gather in a conference like this, we become carriers of dialogue more and more.

Speaker: I've thought about this question quite a bit, even prior to this dialogue. If we start looking at the nature of our existence, then we can truly find out who we are and how we can help bridge some gaps, which on the surface present as differences.

Speaker: I am thinking about triggers. What are my triggers? What makes me who I am? What experience am I having right now? That makes me who I am.

Speaker: I'm taking with me the concepts we have been talking about and the important question of what we mean by the concept of self. In the later part of the conversation, I have been thinking about the concept of ego. What kind of ego are we building, what is it affecting and why we are doing it? This brings me to the questions of, *How can we cherish the environment for all the young ones? How can we cherish the dialogical environment in which to grow up? How can we do that?*

Speaker: I really liked what was said about, *What our attention brings forth is what grows.* It's a beautiful thing to be reminded of. The quality of our attention brings alive the things that we nurture. We can nurture a host of things.

Speaker: The piece I'm leaving with is how a question, which on the surface seems so simple, can be so complex and can evoke so many different perspectives that I had not considered. I thank you for those perspectives.

Speaker: My biggest takeaway was one of the comments made about relationships, and how the dark sides impact how we interact with each other. I think that dialogue, how we use suspension and our own perceptions of how we were raised has a huge impact on that. This is the biggest thing, for me, to really reflect on myself and my relationships and how I can improve them.

Speaker: I'm going to take the buzzword we used earlier, *fragmentation*. We ultimately control how we handle that within ourselves and externally. If we start putting people into different sections and separating them, we lose sight of all the things that bring us together and that are uniters instead of dividers. I'm definitely going to try to do that within myself a lot and I'm going to try to be more conscious of that on the outside, by staying away from labels and that type of separation.

Speaker: I'm leaving here with a question about, *How can our identity be more coherent?*

Speaker: I was surprised at how deep the dialogue was, given we don't know each other. A few of us know each other, but most don't. Yet you shared personal stories and experiences. I think that's the core of dialogue—to share your own personal worldview and your experiences, and to be willing to participate. This is my big question and mission in life, *How to facilitate or help people to participate in dialogue, and to want to open their own experience of life.*

Speaker: I will take with me that building an authentic identity is about fighting stigmatization from outside and inside.

Speaker: I'm in a new role and I've been in it for a couple of years and I'm here to help people grow and develop their skills. I think this speaks to that. I've always said we can learn from other people. So, as I listen to people, I learn from them, and I think it's important for us to be gracious and understanding of other people in their journey of growth.

Tzofnat: Well, I'm thanking all of you for your presence here today and for the thoughts you shared. Thank you very much. See you in the next session.

POSTSCRIPT

What did I observe happening?

The intention of this dialogue was to talk about various layers that create who we are and how we engage with difference. The check-in at the start of the session was limited to the presentation of the names and locations of the participants. Once the floor was opened for dialogue, the participants did not respond to the questions suggested in the outline but rather went straight into a deep exchange presenting insights about their perception of their identity and how they observe it evolving through life. There was a shared agreement that identity is whole and composed of parts that all relate to each other.

The following questions were put out into the open by the participants, *Are we telling ourselves the right story? As we evolve, are we becoming more similar or more different from each other? What are the triggers that make us who we are? How do we see and address the dark sides, those feelings that nurture frustration and violence? How do we engage with people that do not want to relate?*

The dialogue session was an uninterrupted flow joining personal insights with the questions people were seeking answers for. There was no storytelling. The storyline emerging through the various comments focused on a search for a coherent identity. The participants talked about a self that faces its own dark sides and the capacity to engage with others in a peaceful way. There was a common understanding that we decide how we handle fragmentation. Through our self-awareness we can influence what we want to grow.

It was truly enjoyable to witness how the group took ownership of the content. The preparation of the outline was based on an approach to identify different parts in ourselves. However, the group preferred to look at identity from a perspective of integrating diverse and sometimes contradicting parts rather than joining fragmented parts.

Looking back at the session, it was surprising how the group of participants prioritised looking at wholeness. Unlike many encounters that start with the expression of frustration about the state of the world, this group did not spend any time talking about what divides us. That provided a constructive and positive outlook from the very beginning.

In my experience a good way to start a conversation about identity is often reflecting on the various elements that makes us who we are. However, this group was composed of people who were very self-aware and reflective. They were able to go deep without any warm-up.

I took away a new appreciation of identity markers, seeing them as opportunities rather than dividing elements that need to be brought together.

Section Two

Participatory Dialogues: Subcultural Groups (Us)

The modern era could be called the age of social fragmentation. Different groupings of people have very different storylines, in a world that has no viable collective story about its future. Three Participatory Dialogues explored this subcultural dislocation: in the public arena regarding US policing; in organizations in general; and for individuals who find themselves no longer belonging to their own cultural community.

Jennie Amison *and* **Sharon Burgess** *took the bull by the horns to raise the rights and wrongs of the public outrage about deaths in US policing practice. They successfully facilitated a Dialogue, not a Debate. People stood in each other's shoes as one participant revealed she was the wife of a police officer. The shallowness of opinion formed by social media gave way to the complexity of the situation.*

Qingmian Chen *and* **Elisabeth Razesberger** *explored the challenge of returning home after living abroad and away from family for some years. They noted ways people may no longer understand or belong to their own culture. The story of one's identity has changed and there is the inevitable question of how to adapt to the situation given the changed identity.*

Peter Garrett *and* **Thomas Köttner** *explored subcultural interfaces as a break in the flow of communication. There were concerns about the imposition of one culture on another, as may have been attempted in Iran. Mainly, though, what was revealed was an interest in discovering what each subculture contributes, in order to address the fears between them and incorporate their different stories into a commonly enriched and inclusive one.*

Should Police Officers after the Wrongful Death of a Citizen Have Qualified Immunity?

Jennie Amison and Sharon Burgess

Pre-Conference Description

Sadly, the trend of fatal police shootings in the United States seems to only be increasing, with a total 631 civilians having been shot, 58 of whom were Black, as of August 1, 2022. In 2021, there were 1,055 fatal police shootings, and in 2020 there were 1,020 fatal shootings.

Additionally, the rate of fatal police shootings among Black Americans was much higher than that for any other ethnicity, standing at 40 fatal shootings per million of the population as of August 2022. In recent years, particularly since the fatal shooting of Michael Brown in Ferguson, Missouri in 2014, police brutality has become a hot-button issue in the United States.

The number of homicides committed by police in the United States is often compared to those in countries such as England, where the number is significantly lower.

CHECK-OUT

Jennie: What will you take with you from this dialogue that we've just had?

Speaker: My takeaway is hearing someone saying that in discussions with her husband, there's no place where they don't have dialogue. I started thinking about everything that was said about the officers. We're not police officers but we do still have daily responsibilities with our families and home issues with our children. I was thinking that if dialogue could be part of the initial training, it also forms a safe place and an outlet to release some of those personal pressures. Because if you have someone on the job who's going through a divorce, or who's in a custody battle or even had someone killed by an officer, you know they are bringing these things to work. If they're never able to release or talk about it or have a safe place to share, when they get in a situation their mind may not be on that situation to make the best decision. Although we look to them to keep us safe and serve, a lot of them may have all the other components of life that we have. We expect more of them because they're trained but it's hard to train a mindset or a personal situation, particularly if they're never able to talk about how to balance personal life with going out into the street every day to help someone else. That's a tough battle. My takeaway is that dialogue would be very impactful if it could be part of their initial training.

Speaker: I now have a different view of both sides, that of the officers as well as the possible victims. Because of what was said, I am thinking about what the family members of police officers go through—and not just the family members but also the actual police officers.

Speaker: I knew that this forum would be thought provoking, which it was, and I'm so grateful for that. I commend someone for sharing with us the fact that their husband is a police officer, and I will be praying for him and your family, that he stays safe. I just had so many *aha moments*, throughout. It's going to continue to be a thought-provoking subject because of the times that we live in.

Speaker: This is an even more complex issue than I originally thought, and I think there are a lot of avenues from which we can approach it and try to make it better. I have to go back and figure out what my role can be in that process. Where I can help to make a change through dialogue, through my contacts with my co-workers and through my civic organizations, through my board of supervisors, things like that. Will I become a more active citizen? I hope I will. I will put my voice out there in that forum in my local community.

Speaker: This was a really awesome, thought-provoking session. What really stuck out is being proactive rather than reactive in our communities. That's something that, for me, has been a common theme across all the sessions that I've been to in this conference. It's causing me to think of ways that I can be more proactive and even ways that I could educate my probationers on knowing their rights or knowing to ask for Crisis Intervention Team (CIT)-trained officers. I'm really thinking about that proactive rather than reactive piece—to avoid situations where qualified immunity would even need to be an option.

Speaker: I take away your voices, all your voices. But at this moment I have a question in my mind. I'm thinking, *What is the difference between an officer's wrong and a physician's wrong?* While both of them may cause death, do we really forgive the physician's wrong more easily than the police officer's wrong?

Speaker: I didn't really know too much about the immunity part because I didn't really hear too much about it. But hearing everybody's view, it's just a lot to process. I don't think it should happen because they should be held responsible, but it is just a lot for me. Gun violence in itself is just a lot right now. And I take away the fact that everybody has different opinions and it's good to hear and know that everybody has an opinion on it.

Speaker: The community I live in is a small township, Farmville, and I have conversations with the chief of police and the sheriff of the county because I know both of them well. I want to talk about the power of dialogue and if they're already doing it, give them the resources if they need additional help. I've noticed the departments in my area, and in other areas, are getting younger staff and they may not understand the things that we do. So, this has empowered me to have that conversation.

Speaker: What I'll take away is that we have to be the change agents. We must be willing to have these crucial conversations with the people that we interact with, either on a daily basis or just in our lives in general. For instance, social media. It was said that social media is negative, but it can be positive. When we see instances where people may be lashing out and may not be willing to understand the full incident, we can just step forward and try to use some of the practices to get the conversation moving in a positive direction.

Speaker: I thought it was very interesting to hear all the voices in the room. I feel like we have a lot of work to do, and I'm up for the challenge. I dialogue with my husband daily and I am just very interested to see what type of change we can actually make together.

Speaker: Well, I think it was great. There's a lot of perspectives, and that's how all complex issues are.

Speaker: I'm very grateful to everyone in the room who has spoken up and really put different sides of this issue out there. What I'm taking is the fact that I am very happy to be a part of a group that could speak about this and see it from start to finish. Not getting overly emotional and checking out, because *hot-button issues* tend to not work around people that haven't had our training. We've been able to do this from start to finish where a lot of people would want to debate or form a faction with those who think like they do, and then they don't like to cross lines and talk to people who have different opinions. So, the fact that I was been a part of this was just a privilege in its in itself.

Speaker: It's such a huge topic. It's a lot more complex than can be discussed in an hour and a half. There are so many different takeaways. I'm more of a preventive maintenance person, and in order to prevent this from happening in the first place the officers in the communities and the schools need to get to know the kids in schools and in their communities as they're growing and developing. Not allowing social media to form your opinion right away. Letting the situation develop, letting information come up before you form your opinion. And realizing that an officer's job is very difficult. Each one has a different threat level based on their own personal experiences and where they are.

Speaker: I've been listening. I was one of the people who wanted to gain more knowledge about qualified immunity. I know it was mentioned about it being civil. I'm gaining a lot of knowledge about the topic, but I feel that everybody's perspective is important. It's not just one-sided but I also feel if you sign up to do a certain job there should be some type of accountability. As far as them getting immunity, I'm a little on the fence about that. But what I take away today is to be open-minded and to look at everybody's different sides.

Speaker: We need to work together with all the different components of law enforcement. We need to re-establish relationships, be more proactive. One of the best takeaways from today is not only to listen to other people but to take other perspectives into account and not be biased. Sometimes the police tend to be a little *us and them*. Let's make it, *us together* and put the community back together. I would strongly encourage everyone, if you get an opportunity, to go on a citizen ride and actually go on some of the calls. I think mental health also plays a key component. We have more mental health needs here in Virginia. Our state hospitals are closed. We need to get those services back and remove the stigma from mental health for law enforcement because if any police officer tells you that they *don't* have PTSD that's scary because, with the amount of trauma they see, they've got to have PTSD. We need to have services in place for them too.

Speaker: Thank you. I want to start by thanking you for helping me understand what it's like being a citizen in the US, and I think this is a growing problem, globally. I think the power of dialogue can help with some of the issues if we work from top to bottom. We can work with governments; we can work with politics because it doesn't change if small suburbs and areas change but the government doesn't.

Sharon: Thank you all so much for the wonderful conversation. This is just the beginning. Miss Amison and I are Accredited Professional Dialogue Practitioners and facilitators. This is a great place for us to be. And we have a fellow Dialogue Practitioner whose husband is a police officer. So I see some work ahead for us.

Jennie: Yes. Thank you all so much for participating and your voice is being heard and I feel like we did a great job thinking and talking together.

POSTSCRIPT

Sharon: We were excited to have the opportunity to facilitate a participatory dialogue for two reasons, one, to engage in a controversial topic, which has been weighing heavy on my heart, and, two, to see dialogue in action regarding such a controversial topic. There have been a number of fatal shootings in the United States by police officers without just cause and yet they were protected by Qualified Immunity. Communities started talking about de-funding the police and this brought about a lot of racial tension, political tension and a divide among citizens.

   Since this year's conference theme was Dialogue as Story, and having a diverse group of participants from all over the world, I felt this was a great opportunity to dig in. I did, however, have several fears, exposing what happens in the United States; how other countries would perceive us; and maintaining suspension while others shared their voice.

   Several things happened during this dialogue, for example, I was able to suspend judgment when others' voices were not the same as mine—and I noticed how freely others opened up and shared their views. One amazing thing happened during the dialogue; a lady shared that her husband was a police officer. This added a whole new perspective to the dialogue, namely the officers' and a family member's feelings on the topic.

   We had a chance to hear her story and believe it or not I had somewhat different feelings about what Police Officers have to endure. This may have been a sensitive and controversial issue, but addressing it demonstrated that when people are given a safe container and the practices are in place, you can hear the stories that are generated, and which are authentic and real.

Jennie: As I reflect on the preparation for this participatory dialogue, I recall wondering if the topic would be too sensitive. I wasn't sure if people would become too emotional about the topic, or if it would be difficult for some to adhere to the dialogic practices and also feel safe enough to share their genuine feelings. I was amazed that the shared space became safe enough for folk to be vulnerable and authentic while others listened and respected the different views. The stories shared during this dialogue were personal and educational. The power of a story allows a connection to take place between the speaker and the listener. I witnessed a diverse group of people form a connection through stories. So much so that they wanted to continue past the allotted time. The outcome of this dialogue is proof that when dialogic practices are utilized we do not have to delay or fear having important, difficult discussions. I am proud to have co-facilitated this dialogue, which has inspired me to promote *Dialogue as Story* in the future.

With Different Cultural Experiences, How Do You See Yourself Adapting to Society?

Qingmian Chen and Elisabeth Razesberger

Pre-Conference Description

In 1998, I went to Hong Kong Polytech University as an exchange student. In 2001, after graduation, I left for Amsterdam to study. I stayed there for five years, studying and working. I lived in an international student's building and was close to a group of Spanish students. We did all kinds of *crazy* things together, as you may well imagine being in Amsterdam with a group of Spanish students. I had part-time jobs in various places (restaurants, bars, shops, a food factory, etc.) and took a full-time job after graduation. I also joined a Chinese kung fu association as a coach for all those years and learned Cantonese (as the majority of students were Cantonese-speaking individuals born in the Netherlands).

In 2006, I came back to mainland China. I thought I would slip in like fish back to water, however, it appeared to be difficult to adapt to my homeland culture once again. I didn't know how to bargain and always paid more when shopping; I didn't know how to *fight* through the crowd to get onto the bus in rush hour and ended up waiting for many buses passing by, before finally getting on and being late for work; I didn't know the local behaviour code and was lucky in getting my first job, the boss thought I was relaxed in the interview and had a different attitude facing the boss, which fit into the profile of the position; and so on.

I don't know if I have really adapted to the culture even now, maybe I am not in any of the cultures, maybe I am in my own culture – the *3rd culture*?

CHECK-OUT

Elisabeth: We have 30 minutes left. Maybe we should use the time now to reflect a bit together about how the session went, and what we will be taking away.

Qingmian: I suggest we take a minute to be silent and to reflect, and then let's share your reflections.

Speaker: If the world would put the Dialogue Practices into practice, life would be a lot better. I got to know another dialogue participant a little bit better over the last three days of the conference and he continually says, *If we could live in a state of suspension there'd be a lot less hassle in the world.* And letting people use their voice. Voice isn't always verbal. Voice can be body language – it can be many different things. And listening is not always just with your ears. You listen with your eyes as well. So, if we could put the practices into practice, maybe the world wouldn't be in the state it's in.

Speaker: One reflection I have is that we spoke a few times of difficulties in relating to others as well as status quo problems in different societies. But none of that was here in this room. Why can we be here together and say there are all these difficulties in relating to people, but it's not experienced in this virtual room? I feel we have a shared way of communicating and we have a shared agreement to do that. We're able to all connect linguistically here, but we're also able to connect in our commitment to say, *Let's be in the room and learn together.* It shows that it's certainly possible across the globe. This is the most global room I've been in in a long time. You can see how natural it felt to have this conversation but only because we entered into it with kind of learning agreement, for lack of a better term.

Speaker: I follow what has already been said, especially about non-verbal communication. When you get to work in the morning and you say *Hi* to your co-workers, you just never know what they're going through. Your *Hi!*, your smile and your *Good morning* may change their demeanor for the day. I think that it is an awesome way to treat everyone – respectfully, and once you give respect to people, you know, automatically it comes right back to you.

Speaker: I agree wholeheartedly with a lot of what's been said. Respect is really a universal language. People may not remember what you said, but they'll always remember how you made them feel. If everybody operated from that standpoint there would be a lot less chaos in the world. In this virtual room, we came in with a mindset of *This is how we're going to treat each other*, and we knew what our ultimate goal is. It's my hope that it filters out throughout the rest of our department and across the world and the globe, that it catches fire and that it makes everybody operate out of a state of suspension, to get to know people where they are and to have a universal language of kindness and respect for each other.

Speaker: I follow what's been said, especially about suspension, but I'll add respect. Respect yourself, and respect others. And if we want change, we got to be the change agent. So, it's okay to be yourself or be that agent for change, even if communication is the vehicle.

Speaker: My reflection for today, and throughout these last two days, is on what I'm going to call the lowest stage of dialogue. Being that I am incarcerated in a prison (along with brother A and D, and the guy and the female who were on yesterday) I believe that as humans in this situation, it is our duty and responsibility to go into a state of suspension and try and touch someone else and spread it. If I can touch three or four people with this, it's going to continue to grow. When I was approached about taking a dialogue course, to go through the training, this is what was told to me by our warden, what he was expecting and how that was his side of it. I agreed with it because I know to change an aspect of the work, we have to start at the bare bottom and work up. And as long as someone is also coming from the top down, we'll meet somewhere in the middle for change. That's how I look at it.

Speaker: What I wanted to add to what you said about suspension and respect, is listening. Because if you don't listen, you'll miss something. A lot of people live in a monologue type of world. They want to be heard but they don't want to listen. They're quick to say something but they're not even listening to what they, themselves, are saying. If you played it back to them, they'd say *I didn't say that*. Because it's a monologue going on without someone ever sitting back to think about what's been said. You might even say *I want to add a reflection*. But if you listen, that opens up the door to dialogue because you'll know what the other person is putting out there. Say, *Hey, meet me here*. Sometimes we have to lower ourselves and come down to other people's way of understanding and learning, and sometimes you also have to elevate yourself.

Speaker: My reflection is how amazing it is to see how speaking about dialogue and reflecting about dialogue generates dialogue. It's amazing that we don't know each other but we are dancing together in harmony. It's so great, and I feel like an agent of peace, like you all are.

Speaker: I'm really impressed with the thinking together that happened in this room. That's impressive, and it proves to me what dialogue always does. I find dialogue brings out the best in people and their beauty and strength. Who they are. And that's very powerful. I think you feel it.

Speaker: I started with writing these words down: *Live in a state of suspension, respecting, do unto others as you'd have them do unto you, listen,* and it just flowed so beautifully. The one feeds into the other, one into the other. And it creates such a beautiful space. Thank you all so much for sharing and enlightening. As you were saying, *Just take that to another one person and we can bring so much change.* You each brought that to one of us.

Qingmian: Yeah, indeed. I really am amazed by everyone here. I feel your love. I feel the authenticity. With all said, respect, suspension, listening and change start from ourselves. Don't judge too quick. So beautiful. Thank you all for your participation, and I hope to see you around.

POSTSCRIPT

Qingmian Chen

I came to the dialogue with the question, *How do I behave or adapt to my own culture after experiencing a different culture for many years?* I did not have the answer but looked to explore it with others, together. Fortunately, I walked away with some learning points after the Participatory Dialogue, which are:

- The same story can be interpreted differently by different people.
- Respect the others' point of view and try to find the common points.
- Be yourself and be kind, always.

After we watched a Charlie Chaplin video earlier in the conference, which was without actor's lines or subtitles. It was surprisingly interesting that everyone had his or her own storyline about the video. Even though I knew it, it shocked me again how people interpreted the same thing so differently. Obviously, the storylines were formed due to different cultures and backgrounds. It reminded me again that we should be open when experiencing different cultures.

The group was very diversely composed, with people from inside and outside the US as well as prison staff and inmates. All people could relate to the experience of negotiating different cultures on an everyday level. To start with, the conversation turned around observations of cultural differences linked to family roots and encounters with persons from different backgrounds. One of the participants, a member of staff at a prison in Virginia, mentioned the challenge of moving between cultures on a workday from inside the prison to outside, from the free world to a closed world with set rules and procedures.

The presence of prisoners connected the participants on a deeper human level. It turned out how many things we have in common once the dialogue got deeper. A tangible turning point in the conversation happened with a statement from an inmate that, in fact, he felt freer as a person compared to many people who are not incarcerated. He continued talking about being imprisoned in one's own thinking, which he thought was more dramatic than being physically locked up. It made the whole group think, *How should we behave in our daily life?* The common points we came to realize were, to be kind, respect, suspend and listen, do not jump into judgement.

Respect and suspension are critical to living in the moment and experiencing *what is*, instead of acting according to what we knew or thought before. Too often we interact with a person holding previously formed judgments without seeing the one in front of us.

Be yourself as everyone has his or her own storyline, and no one can replace or be replaced by any other. Everyone is unique, like the leaves of the tree. With respect and suspension, there will be diversity; otherwise fragmentation.

What Are Subcultures and How Do They Affect Organizations?

Peter Garrett and Thomas Köttner

Pre-Conference Description

Over the past year, Thomas Köttner (a resident of Buenos Aires, Argentina) and I (moving between the UK, Catalunya, Spain, and Cape Town, South Africa) have been holding a monthly online Culture Dialogue under the auspices of the Academy of Professional Dialogue. We began with an interest in exploring the impact of the rapid cross-cultural engagement that has been enabled by Zoom. The method we used was to draw on personal experience rather than referring to the categories and frameworks that have been published by others about culture. We generated an understanding of the sometimes significant impact of engaging another culture with unspoken rules and expectations that are different from our own. We also enquired into the cultural heritage and assumptions about what is right or wrong, attractive or distasteful, to be desired or to be feared, that we ourselves carry into any situation.

Later we considered the culture that emerges in all organizations, and we began to explore the nature of subcultural groupings and their impact on collective thought and dispositions. Many of us are doing dialogic work in organisations where the culture and way of doing things can be a challenge. A natural extension of our enquiry is into the ways that cultures and subcultures affect our dialogic work in organizations. Please join our Participatory Dialogue during the conference to extend and deepen this ongoing enquiry with us.

CHECK-OUT

Peter: We have a quarter of an hour and if we had a slower check-out, a more thoughtful one, I think we'd probably take that time. So, *What are your thoughts? What's come up that's of interest that you'll think about a bit more as a result of the conversation we've been having?* Or whatever other reflection you'd like to make is fine. Just speak in whatever order you'd like.

Speaker: I don't think that my thoughts have changed. It opened my eyes up to what was mentioned about subcultures being imposed on people. I think that opened my eyesight to, *Wow, do we sometimes impose certain cultures on people?* I think cultures can adapt as was mentioned. I understand that whole thing about coming from one place to another and trying to understand the types of verbiage that are used. We are having different meetings during this entire conference and we've had opportunities to see people from different places and languages – and to see the barriers to thinking, like how long it takes for you to translate something into English. Everyone is trying to be in the subculture of the English language in this conference. That's just been amazing to me. I think that it takes further observation on everyone's part, especially online, to be aware and to think about how not to impose my type of culture on others when I interact with them.

Speaker: I'm left with the word *imposed*, and this idea of rules. Are rules imposed, or are they assumed? And how do we join subcultures? Are we learning the rules as we go along? And then how do we change the rules, and do we want to? I think that for me, on reflection, it is the idea of something being imposed, or something being assumed. It is the structure of the rules within these subcultures that I find really interesting. I will be thinking about that a great deal after we move on from this group today.

Speaker: I'm thinking about what was said about culture, the overarching culture and the subcultures within that overarching culture. And not necessarily seeing subcultures as a positive or a negative but striving to make them a positive aspect of an organization. I think that you can do that by working with the subcultures and creating an environment where they see the value of their subculture in the overarching culture.

Speaker: I follow that, and something that was said about dissidents, and not giving them a voice, or trying to put them down. You do so at your peril because it's liable to have a negative effect on the overall culture if someone isn't heard, and how that relates to expectations being clearly communicated, like when someone asks,

Why do we have to do it that way? Well, it's a prison and none of these people are in here for singing too loud in the church choir. There actually is a reason for them to be here. Sometimes it's an awareness issue, and they're just not aware of where they are! And sometimes it is a legit question: *Why do you do it this way?* And you have to stop and think, that's a good question. Maybe that is something we need to talk about. For many years that was not even an idea in most people's heads in my department. Now it is more that we can sit down and talk about things, and ask, *Is that something that needs to change?*

Speaker: What I'm going to take away also is *imposed*.

Speaker: I would like to say that as a newcomer, I learnt a lot. First, I feel that I'm not alone. And the term *imposed culture* is creating new meaning. It helped me understand that what is described is happening differently in our organization. In another organization, it happens through rules. And somehow the culture informs these rules, either through the founder or the leadership. And I heard very beautiful words when it was said said that a culture is defined by the people. That was very beautiful for me and helped me. It's opened my eyes to many aspects of that. I have written several beautiful questions that I'm going to study more about. Like, *What is the value of subculture in the organization?* This was a very helpful session for me. It will help me to be more open and wiser when I go into organizations.

Speaker: My takeaway is also going to be *imposed*. On the surface, when I think of subcultures, I think of it as something that occurs very naturally, but it didn't occur to me that there are cultures that are imposed or being placed on people not necessarily willingly. I think dialogue helps to challenge those imposing the cultures by asking the question, *Why? Why* are we doing things this way? *Why* are these rules in place? I think dialogue does help to adjust and challenge subcultures that may already be in place and additional subcultures that are being placed on us.

Speaker: I'm going to be taking quite a bit out of this. One piece I will definitely be taking, which I might have already alluded to, is bringing this into the dialogues that I facilitate here in my company and community. I really do want to invite an exploration of the subcultures that are here. We've never, as far as I know, ever sat in a circle and talked about that – and identified them, named them and asked ourselves, *What is their value?* So, that's one of the notes I have on my task list, which is getting longer after these past few days!

Speaker: I'm also very motivated to introduce into dialogues the idea of subcultures. First of all, I like what was said, that communication is key. And understanding that there is a general culture, with subcultures within it. But what you said – *to go beyond that and to name them.* Pointing out, *What are you afraid of? Do you feel recognized?* I'm very new to the world of dialogue, so I might have to practice for a little bit – but thank you all for the inspiration.

Speaker: A great conversation! I got a lot out of it. I like the questions that were asked. One of the things I would like to do, within the subcultures, is to find out what value they bring – and also to figure out what's the fear. Why won't you speak up? What is it that's holding you back from letting people know how you feel in your subculture? Especially, being in management, I think sometimes people have a fear of speaking what they really feel, for different reasons. But I think it's very important for people to feel comfortable and be willing to share what is important to their subculture. Maybe line staff may have a subculture – well, we want to know what their subculture is so we can help things get better. I am thinking about breaking down those walls, breaking down those barriers, and figuring out some things about subcultures outside of my own subculture.

Thomas: I follow and say that this has been a beautiful space for me today. I asked myself if psychiatrists are actually a smaller version of the culture, or are they innovators in a system? The word *courage* came to me. *What are the fears between cultures? And the fears in cultures about the subcultures?* This has been going around in my head for quite some time now. I really want to pay more attention to that. Is the history of the world not a history of fear? What I've seen throughout the whole convention are some dialogues referring to the histories we hold, because they give us security. There is a factor of fear of exploring other histories and letting go of our own in order to maybe endorse or embrace other histories and stories. So, as was said, I take away a lot of questions to reflect on. Thank you all for being here and sharing this space. It was beautiful.

Peter: Yes, I echo that. Thank you for your part in the dialogue. The image that I'm left with is that organizations fragment. They're so effective because of hierarchy, because of specialization and because of concentrated geographic locations. That is why organizations are so effective. But they are also inherently fragmented for the same reasons. I think it's a bit like water. When water is flowing, it's fresh and clean. The water that isn't flowing, that stops in a backwater, starts to get a bit murky, a bit muddy. Different things start to happen in the water. Subcultures are inevitable in organizations. Some of them are backwaters that are just not very pleasant. They are water that's not moving. I have no doubt that the requirement is for the water to flow and to move freely through all the areas, and then they are not a problem.

I like the questions that were raised asking what the value is of each subculture. How does that subculture know that the contribution it makes is important, because it may not be obvious to everyone, and secondly, the question that was raised, *Why would people fear being open with other groupings?* I've noticed in my work in this field that it takes a bit of courage for people to be willing to meet other groupings openly. I think people are daunted by being responsible. It's easier to look at it as not working than it is to engage and take some responsibility for how it will work. I think that requires a bit of energy and courage, and that makes people reluctant to meet others. There can be great value when they do. Very interesting! We've made a good start in this thinking about subcultures and the impact they have in organizations.

POSTSCRIPT

Initially, *cultures* were distinguished from *subcultures*. Thomas described various national cultures he has assimilated, including Austrian and Czech (parents), German (language), Argentinian (residency), Spanish and Italian (language, society and politics) and Welsh and English (in Patagonia). Peter placed subcultures within the context of organizations, describing an industrial complex in Scotland (management and unions) and a high-security prison in England (prisoners and staff). In both cases, subcultural groupings were at odds with each other because they held conflicting stories. Dialogue helped the subcultural versions to be incorporated into a common story and understanding.

Participants in the Dialogue recognised subcultures in different work shifts, where people identify with each other and develop their own jargon. Distinctive subcultures were described within VADOC in prisons, probation and parole, the training centre and Head Office (described as 'a completely different animal'). In food cooperatives, the assumption of subcultural conflict makes the executive group reluctant to have an open conversation with their members.

An Iranian participant described the attempted imposition of culture at a national level, saying that the Islamic religion was being promoted by government, and people were required to follow certain rules and laws. Resistant subcultures were resulting in a very difficult conflict.

This led into an enquiry about rules of conduct within a subculture. Rules may be self-generated or imposed, explicit or implicit. It became apparent that they are reinforced by significant stories that lead to repetitive patterns of behaviour. People proposed that subcultures are not in themselves inherently good or bad. They may exhibit diversity or cause conflict. Do cultures hold a fixed set of rules, or do they evolve? One participant described the entire turnover of the staff of an executive group, yet the stories they held remained unchanged. The subcultural grouping had *inherited* their stories. These stories contained unspoken rules about how to interpret things.

Someone quoted GK Chesterton: *It isn't that they can't see the solution – they can't see the problem!* There are inherited stories in VADOC too, but someone explained that when you sit down to talk with people, they recognise they may no longer be true today, although the history of how the culture developed may be relevant.

In this Dialogue we took a first step into the complex matter of subcultural fragmentation. Organizational subcultures were recognised, and the way they hold collective patterns of thought and behaviour was evident to everyone. It was apparent that whenever a subcultural grouping holds a story that conflicts with the stories of other subcultures, the system becomes fragmented. Also, the relevance of Dialogue to achieve cultural change was apparent. The challenge is to get one conversation to flow across the whole system, providing forums within which all the different private conversations can become public.

Section Three

Participatory Dialogues: Organizations

The successes and failings of organizations are in large part dependent on their culture and on the underlying stories that sustain that culture and drive behaviour. Humanizing the workplace requires changes to both culture and the underlying stories. Four Participatory Dialogues went into this territory by considering power in organizations, commitment to change, bringing Dialogue into the workplace and enabling ongoing learning through Dialogue.

Djuanwa Cooke *and* **Leo Hylton**'s *Participatory Dialogue explored how power, in its different forms, can hold or change the way organizations work. Forms named were positional power, power by association, attitudinal power and relational power. Understanding how these can work well alongside one another can humanize any organization, including a prison.*

Matt Burgess *reminded participants of the commitment of the Virginia Department of Corrections to enable the re-entry and resettlement of all offenders after release into society. The participants agreed, and their views were reinforced by the Dialogue process. Matt, however, questioned society's willingness to allow this to happen for all types of offences. He questioned whether correctional departments are providing enough of the right information to challenge the public's lack of forgiveness for some crimes.*

Kati Tikkamäki *and* **Hanne Mäki-Hakola** *wanted to get beyond learning about Dialogue in the classroom and explore how to encourage its use in the everyday workplace. People proposed deliberate practice and demonstration of dialogic skills. One astute comment was that people who keep repeating old stories about the value of Dialogue are not practicing it. The living story does the work.*

Susan Williams *and* **Shaketta Thomas** *proposed Dialogue as a means of ongoing learning, not only in the teacher/student relationship but more broadly through parenting, supervising and mentoring. The check-out revealed there may be a distance to go for this possibility to become a reality for some in the prison officer/inmate relationship.*

How Does Dialogue Facilitate Mutual Humanity and Overcome Power Dynamics Within Systems?

Djuanwa Cooke and Leo Hylton

Pre-Conference Description

In this interactive dialogue session, Djuanwa and Leo will explore the way they have seen dialogue work to overcome power differentials within carceral spaces. Coming from what would seem like opposing positions, the co-facilitators will show the necessity of creating spaces that cultivate mutuality in a way that suspends positionality and encourages human connection. Djuanwa enters this work as a Corrections professional and Leo as an incarcerated person. Together they seek to invite participants' engagement in wondering how we can create a sense of self outside of institutions so that when we criticize institutions, we remove the risk of the individual.

There are a great number of well-meaning people working within institutions that perpetuate cycles of harm. The facilitators posit that dialogue can serve to overcome power dynamics, rehumanize all people within these harmful systems and use intentional language to further these goals. However, while intentional language allows us to see people in a more complex way, dialogues should also acknowledge that there must be a shift in perspective and action that accompanies such language.

As an overarching guide, we engage with the question, *How can dialogue work to facilitate interactive mutuality and overcome differential power dynamics within systems?*

CHECK-OUT

Leo: I would like to hear everyone speak, including the voices of people in positional power. It will help if you can keep your check-out to a paragraph, saying what you're taking with you from here as we close.

Speaker: I appreciate that there's a lot I'm taking away. I'm taking with me something I shared in the dialogue and that felt received and beneficial. To me, affirmation of collective thinking was alive and well in this space. It's new for me. Thank you for facilitating that.

Speaker: We've come a long way with dialogue and we're never going to completely overcome power dynamics because there will always be people in power. We can utilize dialogue to face those concerns and be strong as we learn and teach other people dialogue. Different programs like the inmate dialogue, learning teams and Working Dialogues are moving in the right direction to get everybody to a more level playing field. We are able to use effective communication a lot more, and we are able to work out problems rather than just dealing with things in ways that we have in the past.

Speaker: What I take away is not to be afraid to use your authentic voice and to identify with people on their level. It's just as important when you speak as when you listen. Try to listen openly without preconceived notions whether the person is in a position of power or in a subordinate one. Just listen for the authentic voice.

Speaker: I've been relatively quiet. As a leader, it's important not only to set the stage but to make sure that issues are addressed, and if there's a conversation after the conversation not to be bashful about coming back and having another dialogue. Following through and holding people accountable I think is absolutely critical.

Speaker: I was very moved by what you said at the beginning about relational power. I think that may be the thing we need to have the most thinking about.

Speaker: I want to commend the unit heads for realizing that they do have power and they do and can control the narrative of a dialogue. I want to commend them for realizing that, and then taking action when something arises that could mess and change the whole dynamic of a dialogue.

Speaker: Somebody mentioned that we will never get rid of power structures. There will always be somebody holding some kind of power but knowing that we can use that power beneficially, to set the stage and level the playing field for everyone. I think a goal of the Department, and a goal of mine, is to move dialogue as a structured thing to dialogue just being a part of the process. Even though we will never be a flat organization, we can do better.

Speaker: I really love the fact that we are able to talk about dialogue. I find that we use dialogues and Working Dialogues all the time but it is different to have an opportunity to sit with individuals to talk about how we see dialogue, how we are affected by dialogues and how we may facilitate or respond to dialogues. Sometimes we become complacent in the way that we do things. So, to be with such a fantastic group of individuals where we can actually talk about dialogue is inspirational to me.

Speaker: My takeaway is that even though I may not have been involved directly in a dialogue that turned toxic, it is my duty to remain accountable and try to contain the narrative. Even if it just happens to be a skilful conversation with the people involved, to control the narrative so that it does not run rampant throughout the facility. That kind of dialogue is not a viable vehicle to perpetuate change.

Speaker: My takeaway is that in my position and given what I do I must be that person who helps to teach and educate people to communicate effectively with one another as well as work with the unit heads and staff. If I see things that are not right, to hold people accountable, and to be a person who is willing to step out and make the whole thing approachable by being a coach.

Speaker: I think one of the key things I'll be taking with me from today is a reminder about positional and relational power dynamics in a situation. If we can create a container where we're dealing with the relational power dynamic play it might be easier to leave positional power at the door when we come into the container. Then we are not seeing people with labels of warden, offender, ex-offender, what have you, but we look at humans. I think it will give us even more transformational power in our dialogues and our day-to-day efforts as well.

Speaker: I take away the idea that it would be good to clean up our thinking about power and that the way power is thought of is easily misused. I'm very grateful when people use their power, will and accountability. What I want is for people to say, *Leave it with me, it'll be done. I'm accountable.* You want people who are willing to hold what will happen. I think we should think about power and accountability in a very different light because they're not going to go away. Either power or accountability. In terms of power, there's both positional power and there's power by association. I don't think that's what you're using. I think what you're using is more attitudinal power. You're taking responsibility and you are accountable for your attitude, and people are comfortable with it. So, I appreciate the way the two of you have handled this and the depth we've gone to in this dialogue.

Speaker: My takeaway is that within a dialogue, power is fluid. Not necessarily just with the people in the room, absent of any titles and such, but also in the personalities. I think power will shift based on who is using their voice within the dialogue.

Leo: This was a rich and meaningful engagement. Thank you for lending your voice, your time, your ears and your heart to this. Not only in this room but beyond here. Thank you for the work that led up to this, and for what you'll take into your lives after this.

POSTSCRIPT

Going into our interactive dialogue session, we were hoping to create a container of authenticity, comfort and courage. We wanted to engage deeply and uplift the need of each participant to speak and have their voice heard and honored in a way that it may never have been heard anywhere else. We also wanted to model the power of dialogue to suspend positional power, level the playing field and enable people to engage with each other in all the fullness of who they are, regardless of their role, occupation, or identity. Everyone would step into that virtual room with a story in their mind, built upon thoughts and beliefs developed over the course of their life about how power, privilege and position operate as well as how communication can and should feel. We therefore wanted to open a space for people to feel supported in challenging their stories and their storylines.

Even though we came into this space from vastly different hierarchical positions within the field of corrections, we did so with a similar understanding and experience of how dialogue facilitates the suspension of positional power, cultivates the strength of relational power, and helps people from different positions recognize their shared humanity and the possibility of creating a shared story. Throughout the dialogue, our hopes and goals were affirmed and uplifted by the participants. A wide variety of identities and positionalities were present in the room, yet there was a clear intentionality to respect diversity and seek deeper understanding and connection between one another.

Reflecting on what people said and what they left our session with, it became clear that the dialogue was successful in creating a common story among the group. One participant spoke about leaving with a new understanding about the importance of using their authentic voice without fear and listening openly without preconceived notions, and we could see heads nod in affirmation and support. When another participant mentioned their struggle to envision a future devoid of power differentials, this struggle was clearly shared by others—as was the commitment to use dialogue to lean into relational power as a way to overcome positional power in interpersonal relations. There also appeared to be a renewed sense of accountability and personal responsibility by those holding positions of authority to suspend their positional power when engaging with positional subordinates. The acknowledgment of VADOC unit heads about how their very presence in a room influences the direction and flow of a dialogue was also appreciated. Engaging in a space where people really saw, heard and felt each other was a deeply meaningful experience that led to feelings of shared humanity, shared connection, and shared story.

When Does an Offender Stop Being an Offender?

Matt Burgess

Pre-Conference Description

In the Virginia Department of Corrections, we believe that re-entry begins at the beginning of incarceration. From that time our goal is to prepare an inmate for reintegration into society. We strive to provide a Healing Environment to encourage all inmates to take advantage of the many programs and educational opportunities available to prepare them to re-enter society and live within the parameters of their probation or parole conditions. In doing so they can become productive members of whatever community they are in and move forward with their lives. We can provide many avenues for change, however, as with anyone, only the individual can change their own behaviors and interactions with others. We encourage growth and especially changes in thought processes, learning to avoid the criminal thinking that may have led to their incarceration. It could be crucial to recognize in the inmate journey through incarceration if, and when, this change takes place.

We as a department can provide the tools and opportunities for change. *Are we effective enough at communicating our commitment to public safety regarding inmates after their release?* We have a wide range of custody levels and inmates from all aspects of society. We have inmates who have committed fairly minor although repetitive crimes and on the other end of the spectrum inmates who have committed violent crimes such as rape and murder. We are to provide treatment for all inmates, regardless of their offense and this presents us and the inmates with specific challenges. After completion of a sentence if the general public places insurmountable barriers to reintroduction of an inmate back into society because of the nature of their crime, this is a disservice to individuals whom we expect to succeed and be accepted into a community.

Certain crimes carry a stigma not easily overcome. *Where do we find a balance for what is safe and acceptable for society and accomplishable for inmates?*

CHECK-OUT

Matt: Did you have a shift in your thought process, and if so, at what point? What did you hear that made you have a little shift in the process of the way you think about offenders in the community?

Speaker: No, I haven't had a switch in my thinking. We have a peer recovery support specialist in our district who is a DOC (Department of Corrections) employee, one of two in the entire state. So, you know, I believe there's still a way to go in the DOC.

Speaker: I think it's the individual's intrinsic motivation. I heard about how a lady told someone that college wasn't for him. But the self-drive he had told him that was wrong, and I heard there was a change in another individual after 10 years. I think it's the individual. I've got a lot of family that's been incarcerated. I've got a cousin that every time he gets out, I'll talk to him a little bit and can kind of see, *Yeah, you ain't changed.* I've got an uncle who's done time and I never saw him as an inmate. He has something inside that will never change.

Speaker: I know words have power. I am a firm believer that the right words can motivate people to do great things. I had the good fortune to be blessed to work with juveniles and adults. So, I got to see both sides of the coin, and words do have power. I think when people ask you where you work and you tell them you work in corrections they automatically compare what you say to what they see on the movies or whatever. We must do a better job. We have to get better at telling people that it's not like what you see in the movies. It's not all horror stories. People do change.

Speaker: I am going to challenge myself more to start putting a lot of these pieces together. As a therapist working with sex offenders, one of the things I immediately tell them is not to refer to themselves as sex offenders. That would mean that you are currently still in that state. You committed a sex offence. This changes how we talk, and I feel this is something that we all need to do. If we are honestly trying to rehabilitate people and send them back to our community as better people, it starts well before they're about to re-enter a community. So, I'm challenging myself to see in what areas I can make those changes. Even in some of the community outreach programs, because one of the things I've heard is that people need support when they get out. *So how can a community aid such support by recognizing that this helps make our society better?* If we support people when they come back out, maybe that helps us all. I am charging myself to do that.

Speaker: I don't believe my views have changed because I believe this change is based on whether the behavior changes. But I also believe that we help with that behavior. Working inside a facility you can see when an inmate has made that change. They start making a change inside of the facility before it's time for them to go home. What we do and how we act helps inmates when they go back into their communities. So, my view is still the same.

Speaker: I do agree with what's been said about the fact that we don't know who our current neighbors are. If someone was to move in, unless we got onto the registry for the Virginia State Police, we probably wouldn't know who was in our community, and I do agree that everybody deserves a second chance. But as someone else said, being with corrections as long as a lot of us have been, we still have that suspicious nature. As far as working in an administrative role, knowing what programs the people who are in our custody go through to prepare them for re-entry, if I learnt more about that, I think my thinking process might change.

Speaker: I think the dialogue probably just reinforced things for me, so I'll say I shifted to a stronger position. As people who work with those caught up in the criminal justice system we can expect for them to have a shift in themselves first, and certainly an internal shift is what's going to move somebody towards desistance from crime. But sometimes people come from backgrounds where they've never even been able to see their own value. So, our role should also be to help them see their value in the first place. To bring that out in a person for them to see that they actually have value. We've always got a part we can play. We can't just sit back and wait for them to have an internal shift before we can do something. If they're not there, help them see their own internal value in the first place to get that ship going.

Speaker: I follow everything that you said. I just shifted into a stronger position. I'm going to continue what I have going on here. I work with human beings.

Speaker: I'm going in the same direction. As a criminologist, behavior is my thing. We do need more positiveness, if that's the word, in our community to show what is done in the Department to prepare the inmates. Especially, if they can use this inmate dialogue and maybe have more classes. Not just one or two a year, but rather three or four. Also, be that person in the institution, do those things that the inmates can see and be positive about through how we live our lives and how we work. Be on time for work and tell the truth. Things like that.

Speaker: I think behavior is the one that signifies the most when somebody's ready to move forward.

Speaker: I follow what was said— it's all about behavior. My mom always used to tell me, *You should always conduct yourself with grace and dignity.* While I do strive to do that in my life, I may not always have done so in the past. I feel like once I get to a point where I can comfortably say that *I always conduct myself with grace and dignity*, then I would no longer be an offender. I would be a law-abiding citizen and a good contributing member of society.

Speaker: I have to say that I think this is where it begins. It begins with putting in some effort to try to change behavior by the programs we use—by letting this be a story. This is a story! Dialogue training is a story. The walks that we do when we do the Resettlement Journey Walks with the inmate population are stories. It begins the initial contact with people that are out there in society. We reach out to courts, to judges and to lawyers. The programs are available as resources so that, as people are released from prison, they can have these support systems. We try our best. So, my position hasn't changed. My interest remains that I want to help people be better. I wish that we could get an ad campaign similar to the LGBTQIA+ population because we do need to have advocacy for this. Sometimes it's hard to advocate for yourself as you know. You want people to advocate for you sometimes. We need to be advocates for the population so that we can change the thought process of how people in society see our people. We can help by being that spokesperson and being able to treat people the way they want to be treated while in the institution—so that they can understand that same process and it can be emulated when they are released.

Speaker: My takeaway is that I've heard a lot of stories from people working inside the criminal justice system about how you see people you come into contact with— offenders—just as people who, for various reasons such as life circumstances, misfortune, et cetera, have landed them in the situation that they find themselves in. On the other hand, I think that the story that society holds is heavily influenced by the media. It is a much more severe view of people who are going through the criminal justice system. I guess my question, my challenge to you is, *What can you do that changes the story of the people in society, in the community?* It builds on what you've just said about publicity and campaigns. Maybe that's part of what the Virginia Department of Corrections and other Departments of Corrections need to be doing. Because otherwise, the people going back out into society are still wrestling with all that poorly informed prejudice.

Speaker: My views haven't changed too much. I still believe, like I said, that there's a lot of good that we do, and dialogue is definitely a good start to it. A lot of it they just have to prove themselves. The biggest thing in my eyes is that when they come out of prison they need to show that they're not only willing to change but that they're going to stick with those changes and be the person that they want to be, the person that they want society to see. I'm always good for giving people second chances and giving people opportunities. My view pretty much stays the same, but a lot of what everyone has said has been really good and will stick with me as well.

Speaker: My views have not changed. I had a family member that was incarcerated a long time ago and it's kind of like he had to get the mentality that he wasn't on his own anymore. It took a really long time for him to prove to everybody that he wasn't an offender anymore. He burnt bridges and people had to be able to trust him again. But now he's a success story. He's getting promoted at work and getting recognition. Ten years ago, he was in a jail cell with family members wondering if he was going to make the right choices when he got out. So, yes, it is a mentality shift when you're inside, but it does take time. I believe that people are ready to make a change when they start to show others that they're ready to make that change.

Speaker: I definitely have not changed my stance. Like a couple of other people said, if anything, I've become firmer about being an advocate of change talk. I think it's super important to help individuals to see their own value. We have people that have never, ever, been told anything good about themselves, and so they're going to act within the limitation set on them by labels, *offender* or *inmate*. They're going to act in just the ways we expect. It's our responsibility as staff to help them see themselves in a different light so they can start behaving differently. Some people aren't going to have intrinsic motivation and they're going to need extra support. The thing I take away from this dialogue is to constantly reinforce this alongside the other staff I work with daily. That way it filters out to the incarcerated individuals who they're working with. Hopefully, it will just start to spread and become contagious. Before long we may use terms like *inmate, convict* or *offender*, but no one will feel as if that is all they are.

Speaker: My thought process hasn't changed very much. It's up to the individual at one point in their life. Is that thinking going to stop driving that behavior? We can give them the tools that they need, but it's up to the individual. *At what point in their incarceration period or at what point in their life are they willing to utilize those tools?* Not only do they have to prove to society that they can be a better person but they also have to prove it to themselves. They have to trust themselves enough to know that they can change. It's up to the individual whether or not they want to utilize those skills, to stop a thinking pattern that pulls them into criminal behavior. It's all up to the person. At what point in their life are they willing to change?

Speaker: I got reminded of some things about change. It's not an event. It's a process that takes time depending on people's willingness to change. Nobody changes in a vacuum. People need resources in order to change. It has to be something that can get their attention, to show them they can change and do better in what they're doing. You can't expect people to change overnight or in two or three weeks. We have seen plenty of success stories from investing in some of the toughest people. You may not see it for a while, but two, three years down the line they come and tell you how much they appreciate you investing in them, even when they were in a bad state.

Speaker: I feel that everybody deserves a chance, and I think the DOC has started to do a wonderful job. We need to encourage people, and the dialogues we do with the inmates help. I think we as a whole are going in the right direction.

Speaker: My opinion has not changed. Like I said before, I believe in second chances. We've all made mistakes. Some of us learn from them, some of us take a little longer to learn. I still want to give people the opportunity to be able to change. I feel we all have stumbled and fallen and just need an opportunity to redeem or to get ourselves together.

Speaker: I would say that we need to find the mental health issues, give people proper education and proper training and then give them a good environment. If you can find out what stuff they need it might help you to help them.

Speaker: I do believe in second chances. I believe everybody has a label. If you don't tip your waitress, she would call you a cheapskate. I mean, everybody has a label to wear. It's up to you to choose whether it's a positive one or a negative one. When you're coming out of incarceration you will automatically be looked at negatively by some people, and it's up to you to change that. Everybody is judged by what they do and their actions. So, when they get out there, I think everybody just has to make the best of it and it's our job to give people that opportunity.

Matt: The direction of my thought has changed because I've been given a lot to think about, especially relating to labels and the things said about the system. You know, *are we providing the right information to the public? Are we telling people enough? Are we sharing enough about what we are doing to make sure that people decide?* We're making every effort we can for public safety, but it is still up to the individual. I really appreciate all of the honest answers and all the information y'all have given me, have given each other, and have shared with everybody. I really appreciate you being here today and everything you've said.

POSTSCRIPT

Unfortunately, Matt Burgess died a few weeks after the conference.

There is no postscript as he passed away before completing it.

> *Matt's good humor, light touch and practical resilience will be missed by many. He made a great contribution to the development of Dialogue in the Virginia Department of Corrections, including this powerful consideration of when an offender stops being an offender.*

We know he would have been very proud to be published posthumously.

How Do We Put Dialogue to Work in our Job and Profession?

Kati Tikkamäki and Hanne Mäki-Hakola

Pre-Conference Description

The aim of this Participatory Dialogue is to examine the role and potential of dialogue in jobs and professional contexts. Participants will have an opportunity to reflect on their experiences collectively. The main idea is to share stories related to dialogue at work and recognise the factors promoting and/or inhibiting dialogue. One angle we could take is to talk about the role of learning, practicing and skills in dialogue in our jobs and professions.

- *How could dialogue be promoted in the work context?*
- *Is more actively sharing stories the solution to this?*
- *What kind of stories should be constructed and shared at work?*

CHECK-OUT

Kati: If you have a pen and a piece of paper, or a computer or whatever, we could be silent for three minutes and you could gather your ideas and reflect on what have you heard so far, what kind of factors you have found that promote dialogue at work life in our job, in our profession, and what kind of factors inhibit dialogue. This can be a guiding reflective question to wrap up with.

Speaker: I think a promoter would be training. As they say, practice makes perfect. The inhibitors would be people's resistance and not understanding the process.

Speaker: I think that people like to voice their opinions and find it difficult to listen. So, we definitely need to practice listening in all aspects of dialogue. But voicing is important also. If you don't have all the pieces together, it's going to be a failed attempt. I think that just listening to everybody's stories lets us know how much we need the whole package and how important dialogue is. And we definitely need to practice all the skills associated with it.

Speaker: In terms of promoting, leading by example as a practitioner is important, and demonstrating the skills and voicing when those skills are used, positively or not so positively, to bring that awareness to the group. I echo the point on practice. For inhibitors I use the word *contracting*, which is really around expectations; time; screens on and screens off—all rules of the road stuff. I think they inhibit the process if not done properly. Monologues, and calling those out because those inhibit also, and not giving space to decompress or breathe if it's needed. I think that inhibits because it raises tensions. And I echo the point on resistance and not understanding the process.

Speaker: I think you have to be open minded, and you have to practice. I think the inhibitors are the opposite. When you're not open minded and when you use monologues.

Speaker: I learned a lot today by hearing other people's stories, but I also have the feeling that stories are not in the present and therefore stories can sometimes lose vitality. For me, there's a learning today that it's important to keep the dialogue fresh. If the stories stay in the past, the dialogue doesn't have the same energy or vitality. It's one thing to hear everybody's stories, but it's another thing to pay attention to the story that's emerging in the moment within the group.

Speaker: I think training is very important to promote dialogue, and I believe the Department has done a great job on that. One of the things I see as a trainer, which I think inhibits, is that we have people coming in with what they think is the right way. They don't want to be open to any other ideas at all. What disturbs me is that this happens even with young people, who you think might be more open minded than us older folks. They put these blinders on and, come what may, that's what they're going to believe, and nothing else can even come in. I think that's our biggest hurdle in the future, to help people expand and open up their viewpoints.

Speaker: For promoting, I have training, modeling the way, getting people to buy in and meeting people where they are. Not using the word *dialogue* and not introducing everything at one time. When I facilitate the training for new hires, I don't just hit it with dialogue. I try to relate it to something like a conversation. I say, *Hey, a lot of these things you already do at home, we just need to perfect it and this is how we're going to*. I think it's important to meet people where they are because everybody doesn't have the same skills, and everybody doesn't understand what dialogue is.

Speaker: I follow about restriction and not having all the pieces. It's not just one skill, you need to know the whole picture. If I then have to go back and say, *Hey, you're not listening or you're not using your voice,* then we can revisit the rule.

Speaker: What promotes dialogue is openness and presence, and listening to what's happening right now. For inhibitors, it's monologue and it's the difference between listening to old stories and listening to the story that evolves right here and now.

Speaker: If we are only telling stories and having monologues about what has happened already and what we already believe, then I think it relates to what Peter said yesterday about storylines. We keep that storyline in ourselves rather than taking care of what is evolving in the dialogue we are having right now. This is what dialogue as a story means.

Speaker: With open questions, we can move from that past and go towards Generative Dialogue. But I would like to appreciate the stories from the past because we have to start from somewhere, especially when people gathered on the same screen don't know each other. It's very natural to start from what has happened and from looking back, but then it becomes very important to move your eyes and mind to the future and forward. Maybe that is the theme of next year's conference. Maybe we gather then and now that we have shared these past stories we can focus more on Generative Dialogue and think present and future.

Speaker: For me what promotes dialogue is being present and knowing what's happening in the room, how we're holding or not holding that container and being able to make that explicit. It's not just the way it affects the group but also that the group might want to do things differently. Even if I am working in a setting where people don't know anything about dialogue it allows an opening for being aware and improving things. The way to inhibit would be to let our cultures of separation reign. In so many industries there is this culture of the hero, the person that saves the day and the person that is right. Creating a culture of belonging and collaboration counters that overly independent hero culture.

Speaker: Just promote dialogue wherever you are on a daily basis, and sometimes people see you and how you communicate. Watching you can make a difference in how they behave. I can give you an example. I was in a group and one of the participants came to me and said I don't want to be in the group. And I said, *Why? What's wrong?* She said, *I don't trust her. I don't think that she's practicing what she thinks.* I then had to put that person in another room because I knew it wasn't going to work. There may have been people who saw value in the facilitator, but she didn't. Based on her own experience, she did not value the person. We have to be mindful that people are watching every day and consider ourselves and our impact every day.

Kati: I'm pleased to hear that there is a lot of dialogue in people's work. So many of the stories you shared were positive examples of how you promote dialogue in your work life. It's very nice to hear and I think there is so much that we can do together to construct the environment, culture and practices that promote dialogue and help us to behave in a dialogical way. We can reorganise our work practices and we can develop our culture in that direction. When we develop dialogue together there is so much more than just one or two individuals can do on their own. It was very valuable to hear all your voices.

Hanne: I'm so grateful to hear these stories, and I am still weaving up the story that we came up with while we put the dialogue to work today. I'm a slow thinker, so I need some time to reflect on all of this. Thank you for your participation.

POSTSCRIPT

The intention of the dialogue session was to examine the role and potential of dialogue in the context of jobs and professions. Participants had an opportunity to reflect collectively on their own dialogue experiences related to work. The aim was to use dialogue within the session to identify the factors promoting and inhibiting dialogue in jobs and professions.

I facilitated the session together with my Finnish colleague Hanne Mäki-Hakola. We had 17 participants in our session. Thus, in total, there were 19 different people from different backgrounds and professional fields and 19 different stories to be heard.

Every participant could tell their own (short) story. We explored each shared story with a few questions and comments. With the questions, we wanted to promote a shared understanding, open new paths for thinking and show appreciation of one another's experiences.

During the check-out, we learned that dialogue in jobs and professions is promoted by training and practicing, voicing, asking questions, being open-minded, being aware and leading by example. Modelling dialogue and explaining its purpose were also seen as essential, along with openness and a strong presence. Inhibitors of dialogue were found to be resistance; monologues; prejudice and lack of understanding; rushing and giving no space to breathe (reflect); an argumentative communication culture; failure to listen and show respect; unwillingness to look at subjects from colleagues' or other professionals' points of view; and silos between, for example, professionals, departments and organisations.

Through a process of collective reflection on the session, individual stories became shared learning experiences. By weaving one's own story into the story told by another the stories became integrated.

When exploring dialogue as a story, the emphasis falls on the discursive dimension of reality. Language is a powerful and meaningful tool with which we express ourselves and aim to construct understanding. At the same time, language and stories can be seen as an arena of action; we construct reality through our dialogue and stories, which reveal our values and meaningful experiences. It is important for us to be heard through our stories – but are we willing to tell our stories in different situations (voicing)? Who wants to hear our story (open listening)? How are stories interpreted (appreciation)? And do we take the time to tell and hear the stories (suspending)?

One participant noticed that all the stories shared in the session were related to past events. In terms of Generative Dialogue, it is important to focus on constructing new shared stories. Hopefully, we will have the capacity and time for Generative Dialogue at next year's conference.

Is There a Role for Dialogue in the Learning Process?

Susan Williams and Shaketta Thomas

Pre-Conference Description

Learning is a lifelong process. Not only do we spend our lives being taught, but we also spend our lives teaching others. Sometimes this occurs in a designated teaching role such as being a teacher, professor or coach, yet more commonly it is through the other leadership positions we hold such as parenting, mentoring, supervising and so on. We all have opinions about what it means to be a "teacher" and what we want our learners to learn. Yet, do we really think about how learning occurs, and perhaps most importantly, how can we improve the learning process?

Learning is a story. Do you remember how you learned to ride a bike? Almost everyone has an interesting story to tell about it. What about your first day on the job? How did you learn your role and responsibilities? Learning is a story embedded in everything we do. Now think about dialogue and the process of engaging in respectful conversations, building up ideas together and developing shared understanding and common goals. What impact could dialogue have on learning when we regard it in this way?

CHECK-OUT

Shaketta: I appreciate all of you sharing your thoughts. Both our incarcerated individuals and our staff members. It's been a very thought-provoking and thoughtful dialogue that we've had today. I would like to invite the Chief to wrap us up with some final words and reflections on today. She is quiet but mighty, and she always has insightful thoughts.

Chief: Thank you. What I want to say is that I greatly appreciate hearing from young men who are currently incarcerated. What you have shared has been very impactful and informative. I did have a question in my mind though, because as you were sharing someone mentioned their age, and certainly, we all know with age comes a level of maturity. A lot of the young people that we have interacted with on the community side and in the institutions are difficult to reach. When I was a teenager, I knew everything and so many of these young people have a similar belief system, that they've done it all. They know how to do it. They sometimes don't care whether they survive or not. Are there any words of wisdom that you can share with us about how to reach such a person? Dialogue will help them, absolutely. Will it impact their lives? How do we help them understand? That is really my question.

Speaker: I'm not going to use the word *wisdom* about administration. You've got men, you've got women. We're not here with our families. So, you might have an administrative lieutenant that be like, *Yo, look man, come in. Let me tell you something. This is what you are going to do. There ain't no if, ands or buts.* That's their word of wisdom.

Speaker: I would let them know that they can have a voice—let them know that their authentic voice matters and that they can have self-worth.

Susan: Thank you so much to all of you who joined us today for this consideration: *Does dialogue have a role in the learning process?* I'm thankful that you understood that this session is not just about academic learning, but that we are all lifelong learners, and trying every day to be better than we were yesterday. Thank you again!

POSTSCRIPT

The fuller introduction to our session read as follows:

The overarching goal of service providers, educators and practitioners is to stimulate growth and change in the clients and students we serve as well as in our individual professions. Learning, therefore, is a lifelong process in which there is a simultaneous paradigm of teaching others while absorbing new knowledge. Sometimes that is in a designated teaching role such as a teacher, professor or coach but more commonly it is through the other leadership positions we hold such as parenting, mentoring, supervising, etc. We all have opinions about what it means to be a "teacher" and what we want our learners to learn. Yet do we really think about how learning occurs—and perhaps most importantly, how we can improve the learning process? The purpose of this dialogue is to ascertain the role that dialogue plays in facilitating the learning process. Vygotsky describes learning as a story in which people learn by creating new ideas, beliefs and feelings based upon social experiences. Behaviors, or the willingness to change behaviors, are encouraged by the interaction between beliefs and feelings in response to a stimulus, external or internal.

During the dialogue, participants were encouraged to share their stories (experiences) in varying learning environments. While many stories were shared, *voice* was found to be the primary stimulator of intrinsic motivation. When learners were able to actively collaborate and engage in the learning process, they felt a sense of value and belonging. Dialogue can be instrumental in developing a learning container. such container development can have a significant impact on learner self-efficacy and on the attainment of shared learning goals or behavior modification.

Participants in the dialogue indicated that they were most successful in their learning journeys when given the opportunity to communicate their prior knowledge, beliefs and frustrations. Their perception of ability or efficacy was influenced by their ability to give input that was valued and respected. This would suggest a direct correlation between utilizing the Dialogue Practices (voice, listening, respect and suspension) and increasing efficacy and learning outcomes.

The final takeaway also included learning as a group process. So often, we think of learning as an individual thing. Yet, in the dialogic process, learning is expanded when the group is sharing together. The confusion, disconnectedness, and misunderstandings—in other words, the fragmentation—that happens on an individual basis is lessened and even eliminated through dialogue.

Section Four

Participatory Dialogues: The World (Society)

Since early childhood we have heard stories about the world, beginning with Once upon a time . . . Without noticing it, we have formed our own personal story about the world, about society and about our place and part in things. Three Participatory Dialogues raised these fundamental social storylines in terms of gender, age and meaning.

Helena Wagener *and* **Jane Ball** *introduced a profound enquiry into the inherent privilege of being a woman. Women often experience the gendered roles of men and women in families, at work and in social environments, but what happens when they enquire into what it means to be a woman in a women-only group? Setting aside the rights that may still need to be fought for, what is the privilege that gender (socially) and sex (biologically) bestow on women? What is women's story of what it means to be a woman?*

Jane Ball *and* **Matthew Wibley** *tackled an equally challenging enquiry into age, by each owning a different side of a generational gap as they together co-facilitated their Participatory Dialogue. How do young and old find a way to bridge the generational gap? They each long to contribute but can find their views being devalued because of their age. This raises issues of sensitivity, respect and confidence.*

Tom O'Connor *and* **Nancy Dixon** *raised questions about how we find meaning in life, proposing this is based on one of three underlying stories we might hold of ourselves. Our core story may be that we are an inherent part of nature and the universe; another is that we are essentially transcendental beings; and the third is one where we find salvation in the community of religion. They ask how aware we are of the essential story of our identity.*

What is the Inherent Privilege of Being a Woman?

Helena Wagener and Jane Ball

Pre-Conference Description

Through the course of our lives, both of us have built an awareness of how being a woman affects our experience of the world. We have worked in dominantly male environments, in female groups and in feminist organisations, and behind it all is also our experience of family dynamics and friendships while growing up. We have noticed how differently we experience ourselves and others within different contexts and we have made our own sense of why that might be. What we do agree on is that it feels very different, as a woman, to be in women-only groups.

In many cultures and countries around the world, women face inequality, prejudice, violence and gender stereotypes – we could go on with the list of statistics and descriptions.

Our invite to reflect on the privilege of being a woman is not to diminish the stereotyping and discriminations experienced by others, nor to ignore how intersectionality affects each woman differently depending on many other influences such as race, class, education, able-body-ness, sexual orientation, nationality, immigration status and so on.

At the same time as women fight for greater freedoms and equality, the narrative can often focus on the lack of power and privilege experienced by women. Instead, we would like to spend our time together looking at things from a different angle through exploring the privilege that gender (socially) and sex (biologically) bestow on women.

Come with your experiences to explore with us what this question means, from the different perspectives/intersections that we each bring, and the potential the enquiry might unlock.

CHECK-OUT

Jane: Why don't we just take a moment to think. Then we're going to have a check-out that is recorded and the public voice of what has happened here. Let's take a moment first, and then we'll speak. If you haven't spoken recently or haven't spoken at all and would like to make a check-out comment, why don't you come in first? The people who are speaking less have got something quite special to say, I have found in my experience.

Speaker: Women are simple yet complex beings.

Speaker: It really resonated with me, and I followed a lot of what you said when it came to having a strong maternal influence in your life. My mother guided me through all the adventures I've been on in my life by affirming to me that her experience of having children at a young age took away a lot of her time for personal growth and being. She instilled in us that we need to allow ourselves to have time before we settled down. I really appreciated that and learned a lot from her. I was able to see in other people today that they had similar women in their lives who were very strong and influenced them to be the people they are.

Speaker: The story, which I heard and would like to continue, is the story of having access to multigenerational women of strength. I was reared in a family, initially with my grandparents and my mother And I got to see my grandmother pour into my mother the things that have made me, I believe, the person that I am today. Without being in that household I don't know if I would've experienced that. Through-visits would've been one thing but to be there on a daily basis, to see that, has definitely made me who I am. Secondly, I did hear the other story about fathers and husbands and the portions they've contributed to my life, and to my daughters. Being a working mom and seeing my husband being there for my children on a daily basis and realizing that they have gathered their strength from him. The stories that they share with their children will be that they have a mother and father who shared responsibility in the home. The multigenerational experience I will forever value.

Speaker: What I've been listening to has been wonderful. I really hear that our relationships with our mothers, our caretakers, those we care for, our peers and female friends make so much difference. It seems like every story had some vital relationship. I guess in my own case, my mother and father were very conservative and told me I could either be a nurse, a teacher or work in healthcare, which really kind of got me off my path initially. In my first marriage, my husband's parents saw more of who I was and were able to move me onto a better path. Those early influences can be so incredibly important. What I've noticed is that my current partner loves being a caretaker, taking care of the cleaning, and that really supports me to be more out in the world. So that has really shifted. I didn't hear too many people talking about that. Thank you for letting me listen.

Speaker: I didn't speak because I was just thinking about so much of what was being said, and everything everyone had to say about their vulnerability and their connection to their emotions and things like that. It was something that I really had to think about because it was something that I couldn't relate to. I struggle with vulnerability and connecting with my emotions. I was thinking about the women in my life and how they taught me not to be vulnerable and emotional because of the culture we were living in and the men that are in our lives. I was just listening to everyone and realizing this is a great cultural difference as well — where the women here are still very much subservient and don't have as many strong role models telling them to be powerful, have a voice, be independent and all those things. I've been lucky enough to have a rebel of a mother who encourages me to be independent and to be strong. I've really had a great time reflecting on that in this session.

Speaker: It's a wonderful story of role modeling, strength, adaptability and even some weakness, but being able to bounce back. That role model can be in the home, on the job, in the church, and it can be male or female. Just accept people for who they are.

Speaker: What is really sitting with me is the emotional closeness I was allowed with any member of my family, my father and my mother, and I'm suddenly wondering about my brothers, and whether they were allowed that. I'm also wondering about the men in my life now, especially my son's father. I am wondering why I take on so much of the emotional processing with my son and how much airtime that leaves for his father. So, there's a question sitting with me that I'd like to explore further.

Speaker: I will repeat what was said about the generational women in our lives, the effects that they have had, and how they have guided us and made us who we are today. I also wrote down what someone mentioned about vulnerability and strength and how they work hand in hand. That kind of was a light bulb moment for me.

Speaker: My check-out relates to my check-in. What I admire in this space is a sense of community and belonging that was created irrespective of differences in race or nationality or gender. The experience itself has taught me a lot. There's so much to think about.

Speaker: I was thinking, *What if this was a room full of men?* I am sorry to say this, but I wonder if there would have been as much dialogue, or what that dialogue would have been about. What you said about vulnerability and strength – that's really evident in the conversations that we are having. One more thing, most men have a woman like us behind them. Somebody who's passionate and compassionate, who's wise and, importantly, can love unconditionally without asking anything back. I don't know many women who have a man behind them who does those same things. I think that's important.

Speaker: What I've noticed from this whole conversation is that having one man here shows that we're ever changing, that you are accepted no matter what and that your opinion matters. That women are not only becoming stronger in gender, but that men are also able to express their emotions and be accepted. I think that shows with him being here. Probably ten years ago there would have been zero men. We are continuing to progress and going further, in the future it'll probably be a lot better.

Speaker: I follow that. Our role is forever changing, and we are adapting and adjusting as women, as our roles change. If the roles were reversed, would we have to adapt and adjust so much? I see more men getting custody of their kids and being more okay with being at home and doing those duties. It just makes me think.

Helena: Just a quick time check. We've got a ten-minute break, so I suggest if anyone who has not yet checked-out and really needs the break, that you leave with one word. Then for anyone who wants to finish, we will go for another five minutes.

Speaker: What I've heard is just great support from women. That is one of the things that's really changing for women these days. In the past, we have been very detrimental to one another because we have been our own worst enemies when it comes to criticising another woman. Maybe in the past that was seen as making things more competitive. But as I've gotten older and I've developed deeper friendships with women I have learned that it's so enriching when you're able to surround yourself with men and women, but specifically women that support one another and build one another up. I'm a supervisor and I'm somebody that really likes to impart knowledge because I want to see people grow and get ahead. What we really should focus on as women is just making sure that we are building each other up. Show each other the positivity in life. Even if you like somebody's hairstyle for the day, you can build someone up just by giving them a compliment. The group of women that I've surrounded myself with over the past couple of years have just been so supportive and have done everything to build each other up. We just feel so much more confident as humans in the world and as women in our society.

Speaker: I appreciate what you were just saying. It plays into what I've been thinking about how to support each other as women, without putting others down. If we're putting males down and continue to function in this kind of binary way, it's going to be the same problem. Do we want to dominate the world, like men? I don't think so. I think we want something better than that. So, I'm thinking about who we really are here, and how to use our superpower, our womanness, our oestrogen, to be together with everybody!

Speaker: Everyone is battling with the same things, to find our place and to be complacent with the role that we have decided to choose. But as women, we're always going to be able to adjust and adapt. It's in our nature and in the way that we were brought up.

Speaker: I really enjoyed this session, and I felt that connection and that unity of womanhood. We are all connected at some level, and I really felt that unity today.

Speaker: As a man, I deeply appreciate being in this space and how everybody was listening and taking in what everybody was saying. It was just beautiful. What would this have been if it was all men? I think it would definitely have been different, right? I think we need help in redefining who we are, what masculinity is and what being male is. That's why dialogue is so essential to open up the avenues of questioning our beliefs, questioning our cultural assumptions and seeing if we can get underneath that. The community here illustrates that. It's very palpable even though I haven't met most of you until this moment. Thank you.

Speaker: I was moved by what you just said. I think of myself as a feminist, but I would like to say what shifted for me today, after listening to everybody, is that I am honestly questioning how helpful is to think in such stark binary terms – you know, male/female. I think the whole purpose of dialogue is that we find common understanding, right? With men too. And I think this assumption that women are all one is an assumption. The idea that we're all emotional and that we are all giving and nurturing. That's not all women. And I just want to leave us with that thought.

Speaker: I've thought in the past that it would just be easier if I wasn't a woman. Listening to all of you today sharing your experiences and thoughts has really deepened my appreciation for our gender and the differences that we're making or invoking in others. I really appreciate the thoughtfulness that you put into this dialogue.

Speaker: I wouldn't want to be a man. I really love being a woman and all!

Jane: A final comment. Men could have come here, but only one chose to. Thanks for coming. I think what shifted is that we established that dialogue is to create a common story, and we have started to establish a common story amongst this group about some of the things that we appreciate. We've found it intergenerationally in women, but also in men. We appreciate sensitivity and strengths. We notice what comes from us inherently as people, but also how the social constraints and opportunities allow us to do things but prevent us from doing other things. So, in terms of establishing that as a common understanding, that's what my experience has been. I think we've started to reveal that. Thank you everybody. Thank you, Helena. Back into the plenary in one minute.

POSTSCRIPT

For this dialogue, we invited the participants to move beyond a storyline of the lack of power and privilege of women that is still widespread in current times in our cultures. Instead, we intended to explore the unseen privileges that gender (socially) and sex (biologically) bestow on women.

Individual stories emerged in the Dialogue, about mothers and grandmothers, their character, and their impact as role models. People talked about their relationships with women within their family, and how the relationships affected them. We explored how we thought about the women in our lives and how this affected how we thought about ourselves. There were many different threads to this common theme.

We were aware that we each brought our own storyline about the topic into the Dialogue, and on reflection afterwards we found we had a common experience and then made a different sense or story about it.

Helena's Story:

I brought a conscious story that women often hold unconscious positional power and privilege in situations and was interested in exploring this with a bigger group of women who held a similar curiosity.

The dialogue, however, did not follow the story I was interested in exploring, and at times the clash between the story I wanted to follow, the story that emerged from the group and my childhood story regarding gender made it hard for me to follow what was being shared. However, when someone questioned the trade-off between strength and vulnerability, the storyline started shifting to a deeper understanding of the experience of these trade-offs, and a story emerged that all of me could relate to.

In retrospect, I could see that the dialogue revealed to me the many different stories that women carry about the privilege of being a woman and how our stories are affected by the generations before us, our own experiences and the generations after us, and how we often unconsciously carry these stories into dialogue spaces.

Jane's Story:

The inherent privilege I had in mind was the physiological experience of being a woman, based on my experience of the wisdom offered by the menstrual cycle, childbirth and menopause, compared to the negative medicalised version in our culture.

The Dialogue did not explore this theme. My story is that collectively we were uncomfortable to talk about it, and, in turn, this story will reinforce my storyline that woman have become cut off from their connection to nature and deeper cycles in the world.

However, I had the joy of discovering a privilege that I had not valued so much. In my experience, women are often tough on each other. In the Dialogue, I found a storyline of the privilege of being a woman in relational experiences, passed from generation to generation – the storyline of being my mother's daughter and my grandmother's granddaughter.

How Can We Bridge the Intergenerational Gap?

Jane Ball and Matthew Whibley

Pre-Conference Description

I have teenage children, colleagues in their 20s, and talk regularly with students at our local high school. Their openness and energy give me hope for the future. I feel responsible for sharing what I 'know' with them but am not always invited to do so. An alternative narrative, which I hear among colleagues and in the media, describes an individualistic, social-media–obsessed, superficial culture in younger generations. **Jane**

As a young person working in state government, I often work with people who are many decades my senior. I appreciate that they have a wealth of knowledge to share. Alternatively, I can tell when my own ideas or perspectives are silently written off because of my age. Everyone brings experience to the table and sometimes it takes a fresh pair of eyes to come up with new solutions to a problem. **Matthew**

Every day we interact with people who are different from us – including people who are younger and older. The fact we have been young, and we will be old, may lead us to be more open-minded, yet attitudes to 'other' generations persist. This is serious for organizations where the young are labelled 'work-shy' and blamed for high staff turnover, or the old are derided for their resistance to change.

- *What ideas about other generations do you take to your workplace?*
- *What is your underlying story of your own generation?*
- *How does this affect how you act?*
- *How we can bridge the intergenerational gap, and what difference might it make if we did?*

CHECK-OUT

Jane: I'm just about to get an insight. It's coming and then, oh no, we've run out of time. That's why these dialogues just reverberate for hours and days to come. We're going to head into a check-out, and we have 15 minutes. As we are a group of 23 it will take some discipline for each person to say something. I want to remind you that this part of the recording will be transcribed, and the words could be used in the publication, so this is a public voice. The question is, *What have you learned or what are you learning through this dialogue about the intergenerational gap?* Why don't we just do what I call a *free-form check-out* – find your time to speak.

Speaker: That everyone receives it and perceives it differently.

Speaker: I'm really analyzing my relationship with my children and hoping that, when they look at me, they value some of the things that I've passed on to them.

Speaker: For me it is about being cognizant of differences – but then still treating each individual as an individual and not as the group that they might associate with.

Speaker: I follow that. If we use the dialogue practices with people individually they will grow but we definitely still need to address the generational gap. It may just be a cultural and technology gap versus an age gap, and we must not be afraid of doing business in a different way to address the changing needs and the changing ways of people in the generations coming behind us. We cannot be afraid and stuck in our old ways.

Speaker: I believe this goes back to the analogy about the forest and having all the different ages of trees there, and how important those trees are in that environment. We are not the same, in the sense of being different ages, but yet how valuable and important we are to one another and interdependent on one another. More than we probably realize.

Speaker: If this were to go down in the dialogue history book, we would definitely have forest-life cavemen and recipes that are not written down.

Speaker: This left me thinking of a Zulu word, and the word is *Ubuntu*. The literal translation of it is humanity. But the spirit of Ubuntu when translated is, *I am because we are.* The Dialogue has left me thinking about that.

Speaker: We tend to forget that 400 years ago in North America, South America, Australia and Africa there were thousands of indigenous cultures before colonialization had a huge impact on that, and this illustrates that there are different ways in which we can live. As was mentioned, things have sped up in the last hundred years, and the quickness of things is splintering us apart from each other, fragmenting us even more. How can Dialogue bring us back together? Because, really, we are a part of a whole system. I think the potentiality, as human beings, is that we can think up ways that are not fragmentary but are cohesive and connected.

Speaker: Something that stuck out for me is being mindful about what the generational gap is as opposed to a stereotype of it, and just having that awareness in any interaction you may have with anyone who's different from you.

Speaker: I think I've come to the realization that I don't like the term 'intergenerational gap'. I'd rather think of it on a more individual level.

Speaker: If we look at different generations in our immediate space, we can use it as a possible learning space – to understand people who are different from us. We are saying generations are different and they have a different kind of lifestyle culture. If we can use that difference as a way to learn about people, then we can extrapolate that to learn about different cultures and to accept and tolerate different cultures. This is a big learning for me.

Speaker: I think Dialogue and communication is the key to everything. That's how you will learn from others, and not having a misconception based on your belief, which might not be what they intended. Communicating and not being afraid to look are very important.

Speaker: Hearing the stories that folks have and hearing the multiple things that make somebody who they are, from the year they were born to the context and the environment that led to the individual person being themselves.

Speaker: You have expanded my thinking. What's sitting with me is nothing's wrong. If it's difficult, it is difficult. There is a lot of fragmentation at play. At the same time, the richness of getting it right makes it worth staying with the huge discomfort of something that might never be fixed in my lifetime. But I am willing to keep trying.

Speaker: For me, it is recognizing that we are really more alike than we are different. Sometimes it's fear that prevents us from being able to recognize and walk into those differences to try to determine what they are and how we can move past them.

Speaker: I think that *the context* is the concept that stuck most with me. Thinking about our own context and the context that we were born in. The people that we're talking with may be from another generation. What is their context, where were they born, when, what was happening then and how did that form them? Not to use that context as an excuse, but to be open to expanding that context to take in what others think even if their values are different. But be aware of what those values are.

Speaker: I'm feeling unsure if I can add anything cause it's all been so beautiful. Maybe one thought I have is the desire to dialogue more around topics like this. It feels important.

Speaker: For me, it is knowing that it takes time and patience to build bridges. Being patient with myself and with others who see things and believe things differently. Be patient, knowing it takes time to build bridges.

Speaker: I've been working with the subject for many years and I'm always trying to find something in the group that can connect people. Mostly when we hold some integrational meetings, there are more older people there than young people and a lot of the discussion about intergenerational things is by the older people. The question is how to encourage younger people to join such things. That's something I am thinking about, how to encourage younger people for dialogue.

Speaker: The center of my life is, *How do we deal with differences in conflict?* This question is under the umbrella of our embracement, becoming friends with what is different in the other instead of pushing the other to change. I think the center of the question is not about overcoming all the differences but about becoming friends, embracing and seeing the value of the other opinion, the other age, the other whatever. It has value for our growth. How do we do that? Most of the time, once we have differences we run away into our own culture. Turning it into an opportunity is a big challenge for us.

Jane: I think everybody else has gone, so it's just me and Matthew. Would you like me to go first and then you can have the final words to close – or do you want to do the hierarchy thing? Maybe I should go, then you. It's an important point – noticing how every moment when there are hierarchies of age, which we have, there is an assumption about what we naturally do. For example, I'm a bit older, so I'll speak last, or I'll speak longer.

I have this image in my head of the description of grandmother, mother, you and your younger siblings that is like the human version of the woods with the big trees and the little trees. There is difference, and we're all human but different. We're absolutely different. Hallelujah! We are different. But can we, through dialogue, be together in a relationship? Be more like the wood with different trees—rather than skyscrapers where a big skyscraper casts a shadow over a small building, and you get no light and it's always cold because they're casting a shadow over you. That's the one overriding image to me. Matthew, over to you to finish off.

Matthew: Thanks Jane. I picture a nesting doll, sometimes they're called Russian nesting dolls. On the outside we have the assumptions that we make about other people or about ourselves. The clothes that we're wearing lead into assumptions. Then there are people's personalities. We spend so much time interacting with those outermost shells and when we work with those outer shell, we are always working with our assumptions and our biases. Sometimes that gets us into some trouble. When we can move all the way down to the smallest doll, there are our most personal values. If we can communicate about our personal values and other people's personal values, we can understand each other a lot better. We can understand what fears the other person has when there is a conflict between values, and how unintentional but existential a threat can be when there's a challenge between two sets of values. I'm leaving thinking a lot about that, and how to make space for people to feel comfortable talking about the things that matter to them and why it matters to them. And I think that'll help me to understand and navigate these relationships better.

POSTSCRIPT

Our introduction to the Participatory Dialogue described our cross-generation co-facilitation partnership. We entered the session with different perspectives on a common experience – the unsatisfactory relationship between generations, particularly in an organizational setting – and a shared desire to understand how this could be improved. When we considered the topic, *Bridging the Intergenerational Gap*, we reflected on the preconceptions we would bring to the Dialogue both as facilitators and as participants. In our experience, in organizations and in society, our generational storylines are strong, and often polarizing, *this group is hardworking*, *this group is lazy*. We thought it would require a delicate touch to guide our participants deeper into *their* own stories, beneath the societal narrative about different generations.

One of the most important things about dialogue is the impact that the people in the room (the Zoom room on this occasion) have on your experience. As a facilitator responding to what emerges, you are guided to new places as your thinking and design are reshaped by the collective. Rather than arguing about labels, we found a collective struggle for understanding. Everyone had a deeply personal story of conflict and misunderstanding between them and someone from another generation, whether it was their parents, their children or their boss. An enquiry developed from the stories, exploring what was driving those incidents, and how they might have played out differently.

The Dialogue revealed a collective storyline of the desire to be seen for who we are – replacing the storyline about *people like us* in our society – and for the unique experience in each of our relationships to be recognized. This new storyline left us all with a sense of reverence for the respect we can extend to one another and for the intimacy within the act of sharing what we are thinking and understanding about others.

Most of the participants would describe themselves as being of the same generation and therefore the focus was on bridging the intergenerational gap between individuals, not groups. If there had been significant subgroups of different generations in the Dialogue, there would have been a chance to explore how subcultural stories and storyline affect the intergenerational gap.

The Dialogue did provide the space to honor our individual stories and to build a new storyline together, which could lead to different actions in the future. This effort builds bridges across identity and connects us in ways that might otherwise seem impossible.

Finally, our own intergenerational experience of co-facilitation genuinely felt like a shared experience between peers of common interest, that engaged the spirit and gave us both the space to show up and grow.

How Do the Humanist, Spiritual and Religious Stories We Carry Help Us to Make Ultimate Meaning in Life?

Tom O'Connor and Nancy Dixon

Pre-Conference Description

Many questions lie at the edge of our understanding. *Is the universe intelligible; is it friendly? Is there anything beyond the universe? Does the suffering caused by human wrongdoing throughout history have meaning? What happens to the people we love when they die?* Why *should people be good? Is there something that is* me *or have I just* made it up? These are often called *limit questions*. More eloquently, Dostoevsky called them those *accursed questions*.

In his book *A Secular Age*, Charles Taylor argues that our modern secular age gives us three basic ways of working with these limited questions. Humanist narratives see human life solely as part of the natural world, of history and the universe. One finds meaning in life itself without a transcendent source of meaning. In spiritual narratives people have a sense of something transcendent but they rely on a personal spirituality that eschews any connection to an organized religious tradition. In religious narratives, people relate to a transcendent source, usually called God, the Creator or the Divine. This transcendent source is seen as the ground of meaning for the universe, the natural world and all life.

Our dialogue will seek to make meaning from the humanist, spiritual, and religious stories we grew up with and carry today. How have those stories changed in our lives? Where are they evolving to? We will welcome and become present to all stories as they resonate with us in the now. In doing so our sense of ultimate meaning will hopefully become richer and more nuanced. Perhaps a common meaning may begin to emerge that we all share.

CHECK-OUT

Nancy: Our check-out question is, *What has resonated with you today and where is that taking you?* If you'll permit me, I'll call on people so that we manage our remaining 15 minutes well.

Speaker: The reason why I joined this dialogue was because my religion doesn't stay in the forefront very often. It's funny to have this discussion because I don't really talk about religion very much. I kind of follow what was said about a good heart. I let that guide me before anything else, before religion. I don't think they're necessarily tied together. I know a lot of religious bad people and I know a lot of nonreligious good people. Something I've just reflected on sitting here is that religion really doesn't guide my decisions. It's what I think is right. I think maybe that's why it doesn't come up in conversation with me that often. A lot of my religion just has to do with ceremony and tradition, not so much with something that guides me day to day. When I go hiking with my husband, I feel more spiritual, to be honest. It's something I enjoy. I don't think it has to be captured. But it's great to hear everyone else's stories too because it's not a conversation I get to have very often.

Speaker: It means a lot to be in a room full of people with very different views. I don't feel like anybody was judging me for anything that I said. I felt like everyone was listening. I saw a few head nods, which is always reassuring. So that was nice. It can be really hard to talk about religion. Most of the time I avoid it. I feel it's just continuing to take me on a better path, wherever that takes me. Mostly it is knowing that there are people out there who are willing to sit and listen and not judge.

Speaker: Well, although I haven't been raised in the church, I still have a lot of questions about this immense universe. But the lessons that I learned in the church through revival are good lessons that have positioned me well to engage with others. Basically, having a good heart and doing good. If you break down all your lessons, the parables and so forth, it comes down to having a good heart and doing the right thing. I will continue doing so to the best of my ability.

Speaker: I value being able to talk and not be judged. In this day and time, you're almost afraid to open up and start talking about religion or politics or anything like that because it turns into a huge debate or an argument. So, it was nice being able to sit here and discuss this with everyone and hear everyone else's views, and how they live. I think, like Director Clarke said, it is about being a good person and continuing that to the best of my ability.

Speaker: There are many things that resonated with me. One thing that struck me is the paradox that a religion can be used to enslave people or to give righteousness—to do harm to others—or it can be used by the people who are affected by it as a salvation. It's the same teachings used by one for one thing and by the other to heal from harm done. It stays with me as a question and as an interesting paradox to ponder on.

Speaker: If one religion thinks they are better than another religion, another belief, that is a problem, or when religion is used to look down upon people or oppress them. I think the basis of every religion, of every person, every human, is that there is something we all have in common. That is the means to connect to a bigger whole where there is something that is bigger than each of us.

Speaker: What I take away is the contribution that dialogue can give to the world. If we utilize all of the training, all of our skills, then we could definitely have an impact on the world. I believe that traditions of men have negatively impacted the pure truth, which is love. Nature is love, and everything that's good is love. If we held that to be our spiritual guidance, then that will be our connection with everyone on earth.

Speaker: I follow that. I continue to work on my love walk because in my love journey, my heart will be good. My heart will be open, my heart will not judge, and my heart will enable me to fulfil the purpose I was placed on this earth to do.

Speaker: The resounding theme that's come through today's session is to let your actions, and your life, be consistent with what you claim your beliefs to be because when you don't it can be so destructive to other people.

Speaker: I realized that we're all questioning the meaning of life. I am really at the beginning of finding the meaning of life. I don't have so much experience. I'm still at the questioning part of my life. I can say that what I learned here is similar to what I learned from the Quran or the practice of the Prophet. In Islam, there's a compassion to others' different perspectives. You tolerate others, you listen to them, you feel empathy for them. You can sit side by side and you can say whatever you want. I think we all have that in common so thank you for you sharing.

Speaker: One thing that resonated with me is so many people saying they don't really have the opportunity to have these types of discussions. It is a topic that many people battle and wrestle with throughout their lives and yet they don't have a safe space to actually be able to have a constructive dialogue about it. That truly resonated with me. It makes me want even more to provide that listening ear so that when people really need to flush these things out, they have that space to talk and to express themselves. That's so important in life. We need that. And I do believe that we're all interrelated. No matter what it is, your faith, your practice, your belief, I'll say it again, we are all interconnected and here to serve one another.

Speaker: I really enjoyed this conversation, this dialogue, especially speaking with different people. I learned a long time ago that you are not the person that people say you are. Don't let people dictate who you are as a person. I learned to have a good heart, be loving to people, speak kindly, plant that seed for them to grow. And humans can grow, just by you modeling away and being positive. I favor having dialogue about different topics, or crucial conversations on things people don't like to talk about. Religion is one of them. People in different religions don't like to deal with certain issues. But everybody coming together from all the different religions and backgrounds is very good. My goal is to be that mentor, that person that people can come to, someone who is who is approachable and listens.

Speaker: Love has been the quintessential theme in anything that we practice as it pertains to a religion. If you want to know who I am, just watch me walk my thoughts.

Speaker: What I heard was the intent of everyone to do good and be good. Everyone seems to have a really wonderful intent, even if we can't always live that intent out. I hear that intent.

Tom: Beautiful. I was very moved by everybody's struggle to be authentic. Every one of us has this struggle. Where it's taking me? It is taking me further into humanity. Thank you everybody. This is a wonderful conversation.

POSTSCRIPT

Our dialogue began with each of us sharing an early memory of the humanist, spiritual or religious context we grew up in. Clearly, each person's story was deeply meaningful to them and formative of the person they have become now. The diversity of the stories was also evident, even among ones rooted in the same religion. Some had no formal spiritual practice growing up, others had become disillusioned with the spiritual practice of their childhood and some held on to and expanded their youthful practice. All had reworked their histories in various ways and were grappling with how to make meaning of the complexities of life. One person, still attending church services, noted the discrepancy between what members professed and how they acted in the world. It was lovely to hear the variety of personal experiences as we built the container of dialogue that held them all with respect and interest.

Different regions of the US, different countries, and different approaches to religion, spirituality and humanism became present in the room but they all shared a common feeling of being important and of giving purpose. As our conversation deepened people spoke to the nuances and conflicts within the ongoing development or evolution of their origin stories. We pondered how it could be that a group of people who were very religious in the US also perpetrated genocide against indigenous Americans and slavery against indigenous Africans. We wondered if the ways we have of making ultimate sense or meaning in the world can speak in any way to the healing of history's pain as well as our current suffering. In the face of such cultural, historical and personal struggles the collective seemed to reach for a human value of being loving as a guiding value that all could affirm and were drawn to.

In terms of Dialogue as Story, the participants liked telling their stories and the richness of the stories filled out the bodily, affective and intellectual range of the dialogical understanding that grew out of the conversation. The stories carried meaning for everyone. Yet, they also seemed to constrain meaning; they were not adequate to the complexities we were uncovering. So, yes to dialogue as story, and it is also more.

We ended with a spontaneous expression of gratitude for the chance to have the conversation. The topic is a big one and we do not often get a chance to explore it in such a meaningful way. Being present to our common humanity, desires and hopes in this way helped to strengthen and deepen our faith in ourselves, in each other and in humanity.

Section Five

Participatory Dialogues: Facilitation

Inevitably, some of the Co-facilitators chose to pay primary attention to the roles of being a facilitator and being a participant in a Dialogue. They explored issues like silence, loss of voice, changed perspectives, the weight of taking responsibility and the role of intuition – all in relation to how people participate in Dialogue.

Leo Hylton, April Hayes *and* **Garin Samuelsen** *co-facilitated a Participatory Dialogue on the role of silence in Dialogue. They were deliberately slow, soft, thoughtful and inclusive to let silences emerge during their Participatory Dialogue and be experienced in different ways. The participants' experiences of insecurity, judgement, reflection, confidence and so on were placed internally or projected externally through subtle stories.*

Loshnee Naidoo *and* **Shakita Bland** *were concerned about the controls that are exerted by the dynamics of power in a Dialogue and wanted to illuminate and dismantle them, on the assumption they can reduce the authenticity of participants' voices. They recognized that as facilitators they themselves constitute part of the power dynamic and that they have related accountabilities.*

Nancy Dixon *and* **Teddy Gardner** *explored the difference between an enjoyable Dialogue and one that changes someone's perspective beyond the Dialogue. The ebb and flow between what occurs within and without are relevant, as are the strengths and vulnerabilities revealed by using the different lenses of thinking (the head) and feeling (the heart). Perhaps doing (the hands) is also relevant.*

Johann Botha *and* **Jackie Elliott** *challenged the concept that taking responsibility means carrying a load, as portrayed in the story of Atlas holding up the sky. It seemed that the open* *generation of shared meaning, rather than a focus on individual meaning, is comparable to the experience of shared responsibility, rather than the weight being borne by the individual.*

Klas Orsvärd *and* **Bernhard Holtrop** *recognised the inadequacies of spoken language in conveying the deeper meanings we may intend to share with others. They proposed giving attention to the intuitive impulse behind the words, rather than just the words themselves. By slowing down and attending carefully, a different kind of sensitivity, curiosity and humility may arise in a common enquiry.*

What is the Role of Silence in Dialogue?

Leo Hylton, April Hayes and Garin Samuelsen

Pre-Conference Description

The Power, Obstacle, and Need for Silence in Dialogue.
In this collective dialogue session, April, Garin and Leo explore how silence operates in dialogue. What is the power of silence to convey ineffable stories that words cannot capture; how does it show up as an obstacle to engagement when induced by fear and/or imbalances of power; and what is the need for it when a dialogic engagement calls for room to breathe? Separated by state lines and incarceration, April, Leo and Garin enter dialogue from vastly different socioeconomic histories and current positionalities, yet find themselves engaged in exploring the commonalities of human experience.

By coming together in this dialogue, we envision a space that encourages a radical type of engagement; slow, soft, thoughtful, and inclusive. We'll encourage you to share your stories and struggles with silence.

Silence can come about when we feel insecure or judged. This dialogue may brush up against patriarchy and its enculturation into our consciousness. We'll wonder about the impact our gender, skin color, style of speech or attractiveness, for example, have on how we listen. Silence can help us see the drama and roles we are playing. It can help us notice the assumptions and beliefs we have that are taught into us.

Silence can also potentially help us break free and get out of the dysfunctional story of our culture and tap into the source of all that is beyond thought. It can help us see our internal stories and how they project outward and dictate our experience. The quiet can bring us into presence—beyond the story.

CHECK-OUT

Garin: I'm wondering if we can enter some closing thoughts, and then maybe the last three to five minutes we can have a quiet meditation for closure, also in embracing the space. Would everybody be okay with that?

April: I might jump in and say my closing statement. In a lot of what Garin and I do with our clients, we use meditation. We question how our culture thinks about meditation, for one, and how we define it. Garin, tell me if I'm wrong— we define it as being quiet with what is, and that can be any thought that comes up, any behavior that comes up, any feeling you're feeling. For me, that's something that's been helpful, just meditation in the sense of looking at your own stuff.

Garin: I just really appreciate what you said. I was kind of laughing inside because I was feeling slightly anxious doing the grounding exercise. I really enjoy doing them, but I noticed Leo not being in the Zoom room yet, and so I was talking faster than I would've liked to. I ended wondering, oh God, was that grounding for anyone because I was going so fast trying to tell you to be grounded.

Speaker: I purposely took the opportunity to intentionally focus on my own silence in the midst of our conversation. It's been very enlightening for me. My natural inclination, as a born trainer and facilitator, is to use my voice in strong ways and I'm very comfortable doing so. So, I purposely made myself uncomfortable to sit in silence and experience that. My perspective, after having done so, is that I need to do more of that.

Speaker: What's sitting with me is what was brought in at the beginning about nature, and why it's so much easier being silent in nature. When I'm trying to figure out whether I should be silent or speak, I often try to use my thoughts, which is always a bad idea for me because the more I try to think into it, the more I start worrying about saying the wrong thing, or not speaking when I should be speaking. One technique that I've learned when that happens is to just look around the room and notice things around me. I can notice some signs that my body's downregulating. For example, your eyes start watering, extra saliva on your mouth, stomach starts gurgling, you start yawning and there's something in those body signals that's very comforting. I stop trying. As soon as I just start looking around the room my mind becomes naturally silent. There's something about nature that encourages that because it's not caring whether I speak, or don't speak.

Garin: I take a lot of walks in the woods, and I'll just share one quick experience that goes into what people were sharing today. I happened to come across a goldfinch, a yellow male goldfinch, on a leaf. It was eating caterpillars. It had found a nest of the 10 caterpillars in a tree and was picking off different caterpillars as they came out. Then a female goldfinch comes up and lands on a branch right above. And she kind of looks down at him. I'm just watching. Then the female comes down. The male looks down, and she looks down. He takes a caterpillar and then she takes the caterpillar and they both start eating together. Then they stop and just nest into each other. They go back to eating, and then they nestled into each other. It was an incredibly beautiful moment of sensitivity. The care they had for one another was definitely evident. The relationships that animals have were just so beautiful to see. Had I been just in my own head and just walking by I would have completely missed the opportunity to see what I saw.

Does anybody want to share something? Maybe one or two last things before we move into the meditation?

Leo: I just want to share some appreciation for everyone in this conversation. From where I sit, stand and move in the world, it's so vital for us to see dialogue as fitting us, rather than making us fit into dialogue. So, if you're bouncy, be bouncy. If you're checking in, be checking in. If you need to look away, look away, be all of who you are and let this be additive, rather than something that strips something from you—unless it's stripping away something unhealthy. But not something that stifles the beautiful uniqueness that is in each one of us.

April: I love that, and I appreciate all of you. All right. Are you all ready to just breathe for a couple minutes? If you feel inclined and safe to close your eyes, as you breathe. If it helps to breathe in that snake or that rope. Just imagine that snake going through all your limbs, all your muscles, all your cells, even through your bones. It's going through the space and all the bones, even in your pinkie toe, all your fingers, your shoulders, the spots in your back. And as you exhale, can you imagine someone slowly pulling that snake out. There are no shoulds, there is no place to be, no obligation to think a certain way or to be a certain way. You are complete exactly how you are and where you are. You are whole. You were born whole. You are born exactly how you're supposed to be as you breathe.

POSTSCRIPT

This dialogue was powerful for us. Focusing on silence within dialogue seemed, at first, a bit daunting. We kept discovering more layers to silence, and we weren't sure our question was focused enough. We discovered though, that this was why we were so intrigued to explore silence as a story in dialogue. We learned from our discussions before the session and then during the session that:

- Silence can provide space and deep listening.
- Silence can see beyond the words into the story of oneself and the collective group.
- Silence can be a suppression of voice.
- Silence can give cadence to a story that emerges within a dialogue.

On reflection, our dialogic session flowed on its own once we got going. We learned together. Silence gave rise to the complexity of communication and brought, at least for our group, a cohesive story of what happens when we take our time, can move slowly and listen in.

In this listening, our participants seemed to receive time to look at what silence brought up for them. In other words, *What was their story around silence?* For some, it meant to pause before one spoke and to share thoughtfully. For others, it brought up some shame and insecurity, memories when their voice didn't matter and realizations that what they were taught to do by authority wasn't correct. Others brought in nature and how there is a special quiet in nature in which one can be completely in tune with its ongoing interdependent, diverse story.

Near the end of our session, there seemed to be a consensus that we were in a collective meditation. People's voices felt to be a part of that meditation. It was almost as if the quiet we pointed to for our session gave space for people not to rush and just be. Rather than feeling suppressed by silence, this silence was a quiet that allowed people to feel free.

The conference was wonderful. Yes, a dialogue can generate a unique story for each collective group. We really enjoyed the groups we participated in and loved the thoughtfulness everyone seemed to bring to this conference. The dialogue groups seemed to give space for people to share who they are in a way that honored their voices. Yet, our wonder remains: *Can we move beyond story and discover the actual truth?* Or is the very nature of dialogue—using words to convey observations and understandings, checking in with beliefs and assumptions—always going to have a bit of story in it?

Diversity is nature, the cosmos and what *is*. Fragmentation is breaking apart and separating things that can't be separated. In dialogue is diversity. In diversity is wholeness.

How Do We Illuminate and Dismantle Power Dynamics as Dialogue Facilitators?

Loshnee Naidoo and Shakita Bland

Pre-Conference Description

Navigating power dynamics in dialogic engagements is critical for facilitators. These power configurations could result from structural hierarchies or cultural and societal norms. These, in turn, could negatively manifest in a lack of authenticity and loss of voice and hence devalue the substance of the dialogue. Traversing this space would entail identifying the various power dynamics, the location of the facilitator in relation to these and finally crafting mechanisms to equalise the power structures.

The role of convenor places power in the hands of the facilitator. This allows for the ability to determine the process, participants and tone of the dialogue. This power is tempered by the location of the facilitator to the group. Within an organisational dialogue, we would need to consider the hierarchical structures that exist and the location of the facilitator. If the facilitator, however, is external to the organisation how does that impact their power to convene the dialogue?

Attempting to neutralise power between participants is also key for a dialogic facilitator to allow voices to be heard authentically. Moreover, the facilitator has a duty of care to ensure no emotional or psychological harm is caused to participants as these could impact their ability to be present in the dialogue. A facilitator should therefore ensure that they do not abuse their power over the group but create power with the group to lead to authentic dialogic engagement.

This dialogue will attempt to identify power structures that manifest and consider mechanisms for facilitators to navigate these dynamics to ensure authentic dialogue.

CHECK-OUT

Shakita: Could you share just one thing that you have learned or that you would like to work on as a facilitator going forward, given this session? The check-out is, therefore, one thing that you've learned, or that you would like to work on as a facilitator. In the interest of time, I'm going to give you a moment to process your thoughts, and then I'm going to call on people so that we make sure that we have everybody accounted for.

Speaker: I learned a lot in the conversation. I'm not really a talker; however, my goal is to become more of a talker. I do the Learning Teams when I need to do them, and I know how to step up and do what I need to do – but I'm not as much of a talker as most people. I'm pretty short and straight to the point. So, I can work on that a little more.

Speaker: I'm going to make room for curiosity when a solid voice is in the room and I don't want to speak.

Speaker: One of the things that was highlighted for me is making sure to pay attention if a more vocal person is in the room and to then balance the scales by making way for the less vocal ones. And regardless of who is in the room, to use courage and authenticity.

Speaker: One of the things that I've learned in this dialogue is that the way I express myself is . . . How can I put this? Power is expressed by the way I speak. If I speak logically or base what I say on logic everything that is related to emotion or experience might not be as heard within the group, if that makes sense?

Speaker: I'm leaving with *name it, claim it, frame it*—is that right? Also, I wrote a whole list of all the different kinds of powers that were named. They will be really helpful to think about when I am facilitating. So, thank you for all that.

Speaker: One thing I took away as a facilitator is that the things that you might not even think about, such as how setting up your dialogue can come across as very powerful to participants. Just being mindful and owning it. If someone names it, own it and grow from it. Also, I will be continuing to work on those silent speakers in the room and how to handle those situations.

Speaker: I like it when people were talking about how to not get defensive when you get pushback from the group but rather to claim the things that you wish you'd done differently and move forward together.

Speaker: I think there have been so many perspectives brought up. The importance of making it possible for leaders to realize that they have to change their leadership style in different ways and making that possible through encouraging people to speak up.

Speaker: I've become more aware of the difference between dialogues within organizations where people's positions are known and open dialogues where you don't know people's positions and you just see them as a person who is there. I think this gives even more openness to a dialogue. I think we have to differentiate the two fields within organizations and have more of what I call *Open Dialogues* where people's positions are not known and you can just listen to what they say. And if they don't say anything, they may put forward their voice in the next dialogue. That's how we see it. We don't know so much about people's backgrounds and the power struggles that occur because we slow down the process. I think you do it too through using a talking stick, or a stone or something like that. For me, dialogue is a very anti-hierarchical way of coming together to talk about things.

Speaker: Something I definitely did learn in the session was a fuller definition of power and more interpretations of what power is. Coming in I had a totally different interpretation and I was going to say something about it but then I had to pause and listen to what everyone had to say. It was a great learning experience.

Speaker: I would like to follow what was said about giving everybody the opportunity to speak especially people who do not speak during the dialogue, and to guide them to be more talkative and to have more insight. If you have a dialogue and if you don't give people the opportunity to participate their questions will never be answered. So, I try to give everybody the opportunity to speak.

Speaker: I'd say that following up with those who are silent in the dialogue, maybe even after the dialogue, would be beneficial. That way, when you go into the next dialogue you can have some background and you can play to that to allow them to be more open. Also, naming what it is. The obvious is the obvious, especially if you're having a dialogue within your workplace where they know your position. So, call a spade a spade. Put it out there on the table as open as can be. I know that I am open because the staff are an open book with me. I verbalize at the beginning of the dialogue that I truly do care about what they have to contribute. And if they sit there and don't say anything that's not beneficial to me. So, just putting that out there as I think will help to encourage some voices.

Speaker: I have to follow everything that everyone said. Definitely, setting the tone from the beginning of the dialogue and if you feel the need to reiterate the tone that was already set from the beginning and the expectations as well.

Speaker: For me, I want to work on getting comfortable utilizing the silence to get information. So pretty much waiting them out.

Speaker: I wanted to piggyback on what someone said earlier. They said to identify your group. Know who's a speaker and not a speaker from the beginning. That is something I would like to do, and then the part about curiosity is something to add.

Speaker: I'm going to agree that silence can be powerful in shifting that power differential within the dialogue. Once you redirect a strong presence you need to be comfortable with silence while those more inhibited participants are gathering their thoughts to be able to speak. I'm not real comfortable with silence in a dialogue. It's something I struggle with. I try to interject feelers to guide the process, but sometimes you can use that silence to shift the power.

Speaker: I want to be more observant of the silence in the room. Also, when I notice that there is silence because of the power in the room, such as a unit head or whatever, I think I would like to have a skilful conversation with that power person before the dialogue and ask their assistance in encouraging everyone to use their authentic voice when we enter into the dialogue. Because if your unit head is not on board, then no one else will feel free to speak.

Speaker: Yeah, it's been interesting. I didn't arrive at the very beginning, but I noticed a lot of what people were saying was how to get people who were quiet to speak. I think that goes along with what was said, that if the leader is not modelling total respect for all voices and encouraging all voices to enter in then you're going to have power dynamics.

Shakita: I learned that there are so many different facets to power, and I learned from you all in listening to how to better identify them and to take care of them as much as I can before coming into a dialogue.

Loshnee: It's difficult for me to choose what I'm taking away because there's been so much, even though it's been such a short period of time. One of the things that I've realized is sometimes things can get pushed on the back burner. Like I'm conscious that people have different ways of operating and different needs, but sometimes I can let it slip. For me, it's to be more cognizant of that. The other thing that I heard coming up quite a bit is a problem where power dynamics are caused by people's lack of self-awareness. *So how do you work on that?* Coaching upwards to gauge that self-awareness, to help to disseminate and develop that power base. Those are the two really key things that I am taking away from this. Thank you everyone. It was an amazing session.

POSTSCRIPT

Illuminating and dismantling power dynamics as a Dialogue Facilitator can be a daunting task. These imbalances may arise for a myriad of reasons, but the touchstone for the facilitator is to know that the power dynamic is active in the dialogue. The intent of the session was to explore power dynamics that arise during dialogues, including the power held by the facilitators. This was a critical component during the planning of this session, starting with the choice of who would be the co-facilitators. Skill, knowledge, and trust were key factors in ensuring that, despite obvious power imbalances, this power was not misused in the co-facilitation process. The co-facilitators ensured that they embodied the intent of the dialogue throughout the process.

In the session participants found immense value in naming the power components, thereby allowing them to be brought into consciousness. We explored and unpacked the power dynamics that could emerge within a dialogue in an attempt to ensure that the methods utilized were not counter-intuitive to dialogic principles.

We recognized that as facilitators we could not speak to all aspects of the power dynamics within dialogue; however, we presented the material in such a manner that the participants demonstrated through their participation that they understood the process of dismantling and illuminating the power dynamics as dialogue facilitators. A key theme that arose was the value of silence within a dialogue and how to embrace these silences. Another theme was whether, and if so, how, to bring forth those voices that are not being shared. Unfortunately, due to time constraints, we were not able to fully explore the power held by *facilitators* in dialogue.

Dialogue as Story: Reflections

Power dynamics have impacted the story that emerges in a dialogue. The power dynamics have been utilized as a method of shifting the dialogue toward whoever held the most power in the session. That was not always the facilitator. Sometimes the dialogic process is so powerful that it is snatched out of the hands of a facilitator, leaving the facilitator having to catch up to the other participants. This is one rationale for having two facilitators in a dialogue session.

This session highlighted how diversity is critical in the dialogic story, including diversity of co-facilitators. What was brought to the fore was the value of making these diversities conscious during both the planning and the implementation. This is critical to dilute the levels of fragmentation experienced during the session. Naming these diversities creates a safe and brave space for other voices to show up, and to do so authentically. This allows for the story of the co-facilitators as well as the group to grow in a healthy and dialogic manner.

How Does Dialogue Allow You to Shift Your Perspective?

Nancy M. Dixon and Teddy Gardner

Pre-Conference Description

Nancy: We can all remember a significant dialogue, one where we came away with a new understanding or awareness that stayed with us long after the dialogue was over and may even have provided us helpful insight into ourselves or others. Other dialogues we have participated in, while they may have been enjoyable, did not have such a lasting impact on our thinking or actions. So, the question is, *What influences perspective?* What makes you say to yourself at the end of the dialogue, *That was really helpful?*

Teddy: In my work as an Executive Coach and Whole Health Educator I notice that strong leaders recognize the importance of presence, generous listening and powerful inquiry as important aspects of understanding another's perspective. In the process of seeking to understand another, we inevitably bring our own stories to the table, consciously or unconsciously. Sometimes, our own stories can be a barrier to truly understanding another person; however, dialogue can be the key to more openness and making sense of another's story or situation. The question we are asking is, *How does dialogue allow you to shift your perspective?* Together we will explore how the lens with which we reflect and listen influences us. We will do this by starting with a guided meditation that allows for listening through the *eyes of the mind* versus listening through the *eyes of the heart*. We will then have a dialogue about what shift in perspective you experienced in your stories.

Ultimately, we will be exploring how dialogue can potentially expand our horizons through sharing our experiences.

CHECK-OUT

Teddy: This has been a really rich conversation, and so I'm wanting to honor all voices here. There's so much great wisdom in the room that's already been shared. We want, hopefully, to hear from everyone. I'm going to start and just call people's names according to the order that you're in on my screen for our check-out. We'd like everybody to check out with just something you are leaving with.

Speaker: One thing I'm leaving with is to be open for my perspective to change. I know many times that's difficult for people, including myself.

Speaker: I would say, try to look inside someone's soul because everybody's experiences are different. Everybody has a different perspective. I'm going to be listening more to get that deeper understanding of everybody's perspective.

Speaker: I was thinking that you wanted us to see the dialogue through the lenses of the heart. Looking with a heart lens is something I have to think about.

Speaker: I listen a lot because it's a training for me to talk English. I listen to your voices, and I can hear that everyone was really committed to the questions and to finding out how to become more flexible in their thoughts. We all had a lot of time to think about the questions we met, and it was really good to hear new thinking that I hadn't thought about earlier. There is a lot more to think about in the future because I can hear my kids have changed, and I really want to change because then I can be someone who can change with them in the future.

Speaker: What I'm leaving with is being able to be more open-minded about children and being more open-minded, so I'm be able to shift my perspective of how they see things and how we talk together.

Speaker: The notion of pace and awareness, and the flow between the inside out and the outside in. What's happening within me that's then present and available to other people. That's the inside out. But also, what's happening on the outside that shapes how I then react internally. Something about the ebbing and flowing of awareness and choice.

Speaker: You took the words out of my mouth. I was drawn to that in my coaching practice. How to ensure a balance between the inside and outside environment and my role in that.

Speaker: I'm leaving with what we did at the beginning. I can see that I see a situation from a different perspective depending on if I use my head or if I use my heart.

Speaker: I can keep growing. Dialogue is going to allow me to keep growing as I venture into my retirement years. As I interact with others, to not jump in, to listen more, to listen to other perspectives. With the generations that we're dealing with, we have to slow down, take a moment, meditate and take in that breath to allow what our awareness is going to be so we can move forward.

Speaker: I wonder how my mind and heart could be disconnected. Especially with the connection between the inner world and the outer world, the role of facilitator, building a relationship and retiring.

Speaker: In the Department we always feel that people have the ability to change and to evolve. Listening to a lot of people's responses, especially when it comes to their parenting styles is resonating with me. I'm having difficulties with my sons who are going through puberty, and one is on the spectrum. They are becoming very difficult to deal with. Maybe I need to create a balance with that toughness that my mother instilled in me and shift my parenting style accordingly. Listening was kind of eye-opening. Maybe I'm a little too stuck in my ways, and maybe the approaches that I've been using are not the best.

Speaker: My takeaway is to remain cognizant of self-awareness and not lock onto a particular set of perspectives. To be aware of how I'm reacting on the inside and how that's spilling over onto the outside. We think with our heads and feel with our hearts. Sometimes maybe we need to flip-flop those when we're trying to communicate with others to get a different perspective.

Speaker: Vulnerability. As a leader, when you're vulnerable it shows great value to people who look up to you. They see that you're still a human and you're still a person despite what your role may be. You still have strengths, and you still have weaknesses. Self-awareness and vulnerability are the two things that I am thinking about.

Speaker: My takeaway is to slow down, listen with the heart and to see what it means to put yourself in that other person's shoes, to see if you could feel what they are feeling.

Teddy: Great. Thank you everyone for your wonderful check-outs. I'm checking out with appreciation about holding awareness of this balance about what's going on outside versus inside. And so much gratitude for the chance to do this with all of you and with Nancy. What a rich learning community this is.

POSTSCRIPT

Intention for Dialogue

Our check-in asked participants to share about someone or something that influenced their perspective. Following the check-ins, Teddy began the dialogue for us with a meditation on the "glass half full or half empty" and the choice to listen with our head or heart. Starting with a meditation seemed to make a profound difference in the participants' depth of reflection.

Dialogue Outcomes

The stories that followed were varied and heartfelt. Several stories were appreciative about participants gaining new perspectives from their grown children. One participant talked about the death of a friend who reminded the storyteller that life is short. Another told about learning from a relative in a wheelchair. One participant's perspective was influenced by a mother who was consumed with hate allowing the participant to learn how not to be.

Partway through our time together, the topic moved to what causes a shift when we are in dialogue. The group concluded that such a shift occurred when they could change something internally rather than through change being caused by something external. They spoke of the inner change as *thinking slower, framing frustrations as opportunities to go inside to see what is triggering me, and noticing when I can get out of my head*.

Near the end of our time together, the topic moved once again to participants posing questions to the group about how one can shift a container that isn't safe and how we grow our own safety. Some of the inquiries posed were:

- Am I asking the right question(s)?
- How do we make a container safe through shifting perspective(s)?
- How do we put ourselves in another's shoes?
- How do we allow for more slowing down?

The check-out was equally rich. Repeatedly, participants mentioned "the heart," reflecting back on the meditation for choosing to listen with the heart or head. Many participants offered how they intended to change based on the dialogue we had together, stating, *Maybe I'll deal with my sons in a different way. Perhaps, I will be more open-minded. This is reminding me to work on myself.* Others spoke about the joy of being in dialogue.

Learning(s) About How Dialogue Allows you to Shift Your Perspective

Participants noted that during our time together, their perspectives shifted. That helped us all to remember that we learn from being in dialogue with others. Overall, key components to dialogue shifting a person's perspective were noted as *being open-minded, listening for understanding, trust-building, opening the heart, suspending judgment, vulnerability, self-awareness, interconnectedness of (internal processing, external process, and facilitator role), empathy, and presence.*

Discoveries About *Dialogue as Story*

Dialogue gives voice to a person's story. Presence, sensitivity and trust-building are equally essential to the flow of a good dialogue.

Creative Capacity Building: How Can Our Imagination Craft Space for The World?

Johann Botha and Jackie Elliott

Pre-Conference Description

There is a common assumption that to be responsible is to *take on* responsibilities, to *take ownership* of something with all its problems. For many this, *having* and *taking on* of a responsibility is seen as a chore or even a punishment. Atlas, who fought with the Titans against the Olympians and lost, was punished by Zeus to carry the world's problems and to uphold the sky.

If we imagine Atlas as many artists have knelt by the weight of the responsibility, we may wonder whether he is in a position that can respond well to the flux and changes of life. More likely he feels trapped by his responsibilities.

For many of us, our work and family load may feel like a similar burden, which means we are not able to respond well to pandemics and climate change, or any other given situation.

- *Is responsibility a load we must carry or more like being a space of receptivity?*

We invite you into a mutual inquiry and open Generative Dialogue and will share with you an aspect of our work we call Social Alchemy. This aspect of receptivity falls under the art of contemplation as we seek ways towards social renewal.

CHECK-OUT

Johann: The reason we like a longer check-out is that it opens a little more room for us to process and reflect on what has been shared. We can cover the same terrain, or you can process further. It also gives us a chance to get back into sharing your voice.

Speaker: What I'm hearing is responsibility. When I think about responsibility, it comes back to my family. This is my first time participating in a dialogue. I decided to step up because at work I get into a little comfort zone. I am a Probation Officer and I try to do only what I can handle with my caseload. But when I think about responsibility, I feel like my family is a lot of responsibility – so I try to push things back to them. We need to talk with them more, instead of just stepping out in front of them. Instead, allow them to discuss it so as to see what they can do differently. This is where dialogue comes in for me. It teaches me how to dialogue with my family to get them to take care of their responsibilities instead of putting it back on me.

Speaker: I think the thing that's going to stick with me is an image of Native Americans sitting around the campfire and having their dialogue about hunting buffalo – the old story that David Bohm gave us. It was just a free-form conversation, but they were talking about the buffalo hunt the next day. I would love to sit around a campfire with you all and to be talking about whatever we're going to get up and do the next day and have it all come together because we're sharing what we want to be doing.

Speaker: What I'm going to take away from this is if there's something that needs doing – which we might call responsibility – and we're talking about it in a dialogical context it is fun. But if it's given to us from the top down, it may not be fun. I immediately felt when we asked, *What do you feel, see, think when you hear responsibility?* Throughout the conversation, I realised that the things I feel responsible for are things that I care about, and I think that's what makes it heavy. I take this responsibility seriously. The dialogue kind of reframed it for me.

Speaker: What I've taken here is that if I use the dialogical principles, I would be able to connect with people and lessen my burden in what I'm doing and that will help me to stay healthy.

Speaker: I'm a mindfulness practitioner and I've been thinking about how Buddhist philosophy can play into this idea of responsibility. The basic idea behind Buddhist philosophy is, *How do we reduce suffering?* Perhaps responsibility and feeling burdensome is a form of suffering. Another thing that came up for me from Buddhist philosophy was the idea of loving kindness. With loving kindness, you first start by offering loving kindness to yourself. Maybe it's sort of like the airplane safety videos. Help yourself first before you help the person next to you. The idea is that you start with loving kindness for yourself but then you extend it out. We need to offer ourselves loving kindness and then we need to offer everyone else loving kindness. And in doing so, the hope is that we reduce suffering in some way.

Speaker: I'm not quite ready for checking out because it's still moving a lot in me. The only thing that helps me out a little bit is believing that although we all have different experiences we are not in this alone. That of course has a lot to do with my story and why I love dialogue. I guess it's about coherence. A sense of coherence in relational gatherings and helping each other out. Being in one room with the ones that are healed and the ones that are hurting and bringing all those voices together. That's what I hope for when I do dialogue.

Jackie: I think that there have been so many different things that we've talked about today that I'm still processing. I do think being mindful even of how we portray receiving responsibility to others is so important. One of the things we talked about is, *How does it make someone feel when you're passing on responsibility? Are we being mindful in how we're sharing our levels of responsibility?*

POSTSCRIPT

Dialogue has many dimensions that range from sharing meaning and participatory inquiry to a collective form of meditation. To narrow our inquiry, we selected the concept of responsibility and tried to evoke the images, stories and sense-makings around the myths and stories we tell ourselves about responsibility.

There is a common assumption that to be responsible is to take on responsibilities, to take ownership of something with all of its problems. We tracked this idea back to the myth of Atlas, who fought alongside the Titans against Zeus, lost and was subsequently punished by Zeus to uphold the sky. Many artists have imagined Atlas as knelt down by the weight of responsibility as if he is trapped by his obligations. The very idea of the sky became a globe and with it a load to carry on our shoulders. But is responsibility a load we must carry? Are there other ways to imagine it? Through dialogue and the use of our imagination, we can inquire into the images and stories that responsibility conjures up for us as a group and see if those images are coherent, and if new images may yield new insights.

Reflections from the facilitators

During the check-out, we could see that some of the group participants were weavers, sense-makers and storytellers who were naturally drawn to unify fragments of conversation in an attempt to construct a meaningful image. There seems to be a human preference to construct meaning, rather than open to all the ways in which our thinking may be incoherent. It could be that we are natural meaning-makers rather than being automatically inclined to inquire into the incoherence of our efforts to construct images of ourselves and the world.

We were reminded of the Dialogical principle to share into the middle of the circle (the open space between us) rather than addressing specific persons. We have the capacity to be that open space and to wonder about different perspectives, without a need to cling or solidify one aspect of a story or narrative. This capacity to function as an open space of receptibility is where new insight, images and stories may emerge from, and this is what we mean by imagination. Imagination can turn to fantasy when we move away from this open ability to shift between perspectives and keep solidifying a single narrative/identity or perspective.

It seems a kind of truth that we have a need to feel significant and have meaning in our lives to make it worth living. The process we call Social Alchemy is the dialogical work of finding harmony between our need to solidify a sense of self – to concretize meaning – and the ability to dissolve and be able to be receptive to various perspectives, to see our own incoherence.

A key focus of ours that needs much more exploration is the capacity of imagination (as an image of openness) to enable us to flow with shared meaning rather than fixate on individual meaning.

What Can We Learn by Thinking of Dialogue as Exploring Intuitions Together?

Klas Orsvärd and Bernhard Holtrop

Pre-Conference Description

One thing I like about dialogue is that it takes us to a place where we communicate at a deeper and richer level than can be captured in words. It can enable us to explore topics that are too complex to understand precisely.

> *Can we inspire and encourage that richer level of communication by thinking of dialogue as exploring intuitions together?*

I use the word *intuition* here in the following way. Before you express a thought verbally, you have a non-verbal intuition that you want to share. You try to do that by expressing some of the intuition in words. If I ask, *What do you mean by that?* you have to dig deeper into your intuition to try to give me better clues and it might take a longer conversation. In dialogue, the responses you get will probably change your intuitions. Our intuitions influence each other. In other words, we are thinking together.

If we think of dialogue as exploring intuitions together,

- Can it make us more curious about what the other person means?
- Can it make us more humble about our own opinions?
- Can it help us find common ground?
- Can it help us better understand our own intuitions and revise them?
- Can it encourage us to spend more time contemplating topics non-verbally?

Does this view of dialogue resonate with your experience? Can you help me explore this intuition about dialogue?

CHECK-OUT

Klas: We only have 10 minutes left, unfortunately. We have been instructed to have a mandatory check-out, and that check-out is going to be used for harvesting, in order to produce the written proceedings of the conference. I would like everyone to reflect for a minute on what you would like to share, from this session, as your check-out.

Speaker: Somehow the idea arose, although it is not a new idea, that we cannot escape communication, and dialogue is what makes that communication occasionally tolerable. Much of it is not very responsible. So, dialogue is a way of, together, making it more responsible and more tolerable and even worthwhile.

Speaker: This reminded me of something I'm always struck by. You know how you continue to be struck by something because it's so strange? We have limited the human potential and capacity for communication by the way we communicate in the world. Even the formality of dialogue, as some people teach it, and how many nonverbal forces and worlds there are for us to explore and bring to productive conversations. It just amazes me. I say, *Wow, there's so much more*. I appreciate very much that you started to dig into that unseen world for us, using the word intuition.

Speaker: I joined a session yesterday, where we were invited to consider the path that we would follow if there was no leader to follow, and most of the conversation was about leadership. It was only after we closed that I really thought, and I had my most original thought when everybody had gone home. I thought the problem with the inquiry about what path I would follow was the word *path*. It was structuring all of our conversation, that the intention of communication was in some way to follow a particular direction, with a goal. People started using the word *goal* quite a lot. They started using the word *direction*, the *right direction* and the *wrong direction*. It all came from the word *path*, which sowed a lot of mischief. I thought this session has been not only judicious, it's also been sensitive and inquiring and thoughtful about the traps and the slipperiness of words, especially across languages. The possibility exists that we ourselves don't even really know what we have just said or if we understand why the reaction to it might be other than we expected because intuition-intentions are not ours to control. Anyway, the whole session was for me an exemplification of how critical it is to really attend to, when we finally resort to words, what it is we're saying and where it comes from.

Speaker: One of the things I was noticing is that the first two breakout dialogues I was in had twenty-two people in them, so the luxury of this small group was really nourishing to me. That's the first thing I noticed, and as we talked both of our facilitators did a beautiful job of hearing what people were saying and then modelling the behaviour that they were trying to nurture in the dialogue, which is so lovely. Then the slowing down of the pace in a way that didn't feel stifling, but rather felt invitational to me, I think that is beautiful, the sort of gentle way that was invited. I think it did open up a bigger space for people to share what they needed to share. What I want to continue to think about is that when we try to nurture this kind of space, when we have the luxury of this kind of conversation, that we hold those tools lightly enough that we're able to recognise that the people who come into our dialogues do not necessarily come from the place we come from. And that the grief they may bring into the room, or the trauma they may be bring into the room or the lived experience is something that is not going to be easy to let go of just because we had a mindfulness five minutes at the beginning (which I felt was so beautiful about the way you did this). You just kept back and invited people in.

Speaker: Beautiful. I mean I loved it. This is so far my favourite session, and the thing that I really appreciate about it is that he was saying about the *path*, a word that kind of was restricting their thoughts. There was no such thing here. We were an open forum. You can talk about anything you want; you have to stay within the topic, but you can explore. For example, you can talk negative, you can talk pessimism, you can talk anything you want. Nobody's going to stop what you want to share. You can express your diverse personality as much as you can. This session was for me very intriguing and inquisitive. Some people just made so many good points, and I am making notes of those points. I would really like to explore this topic more.

Speaker: I know I didn't say much, but I'm still learning to find my own voice, even at my age. Just sitting here listening to different experiences has really taught me a lot. I was thinking as I listened to everyone that I didn't realise we are a walking communication in just the way we present ourselves, the way we enter a room.

Speaker: The way we start a conversation can set the tone for a lot of things. I will keep on thinking about this, but this dialogue was a great reminder of the importance of, the value of, spaciousness. I talk about spaciousness, and most of the time I'm not spacious. I'm not slow. I'm pushy. I'm demanding. I'm also Italian. And most of the time, I want things done. Even though I know (and sometimes I practice it) the benefits of spaciousness and slowing down. I do practice it, but I realise that most of the time I'm not doing it. It's like when you play a guitar, and you want to invite other instruments to come in, you play the basic chords. This gives you a spaciousness because if you play the high notes, you're closing and you're narrowing the space. So, being invitational, I see it's an attitude. I will have to reflect a lot on that. And how do I incorporate that in my being more? I have homework to do. Good.

Speaker: I feel blissful right now and that's, I think, an important outcome of this conversation. I feel really slowed down. This dialogue was a wonderful reminder of how perfectly imperfect we are as human beings, and it is wonderful to realise that our communication is also by definition imperfect. Looking not only at your conversation partner with compassion but also looking with compassion to your own ways of communicating and trying to convey something that you can perhaps even yourself hardly put into words. To dance with that instead of struggling with it. Perhaps something new can pop up in my imperfectness meeting some other imperfectness in the communication. That's what I get out of it.

Klas: I'm really, really grateful for the whole dialogue and your participation, and all that you have shared with us. It helps me a lot in my exploring of this intuition. I'm grateful and happy that you agree that thinking of the meaning behind the words as an intuition might be helpful. Some new ideas have occurred for me today. One is the trap of outcome, that it tends to limit us. Then the importance of how we speak to each other, how we ask questions, how we report back, what we think we heard, not habitually speaking of communication as something very verbal, but actually gaining the habit of articulating the fact that we are exploring intuition. I think those are the main things that I have on my mind right now. Thank you very much for being with me and Bernhard in this time.

POSTSCRIPT

Our invitation for this session was to explore together if we can have a richer level of communication when viewing dialogue as exploring intuitions together.

Language is highly ambiguous, so we always have to guess what another person means. We become much better at this guessing if we remain sincerely curious about what the other person means, bearing in mind that their meaning is not clear and cannot really be captured in words. When dialogue is flowing, we automatically pay attention to the meaning that we are somehow trying to share, both as speakers and as listeners. Our invitation in this session was to promote the idea of thinking about meaning as intuitions that we try to share with each other. In dialogue, our intuitions influence each other; in other words, we are thinking together.

We began the session by expressing this invitation through a dialogue between Klas and Bernhard, and we tried to talk about our invitation in an intuitively exploratory way through our wording, tone of voice, body language and tempo.

We then had a short silent pause, followed by a group check-in with some personal reflections on the topic we just introduced, and we then continued with a free-floating dialogue. It became quite moving to us as facilitators to experience a sense of resonance, using words and yet moving beyond words. The small size of nine people was helpful to this process.

We are very grateful to the participants. Their presence felt like a blissful embrace, as did the words that were shared. An intuitive perspective on dialogue does indeed seem intriguing and helpful. It is not a trivial shift, especially in disagreements when we need it the most. We will continue this exploration.

We would like to end this postscript with some reflections on how our session theme relates to the broader conference theme of *Dialogue as Story*. Both themes attempt to draw attention to the meaning-making that happens in a conversation. Where a discussion is very focused on the verbal aspects of communication, dialogue is more about communicating meaning. One way to encourage dialogue is to draw attention to the meaning beyond the phrases people use but this approach can be vague and elusive. Another way is to draw attention to the stories behind what we are saying and yet another is to draw attention and give space to the intuitions behind what we are saying.

Milton Keynes UK
Ingram Content Group UK Ltd.
UKHW050506241123
433144UK00004B/168